ASSESSING SOCIOLOGISTS IN HIGHER EDUCATION

Assessing Sociologists in Higher Education

Edited by
ERIC HARRISON
ROBERT MEARS

Ashgate

Aldershot • Burlington USA • Sydney • Singapore

Published by
Ashgate Publishing Limited
Gower House
Croft Road
Aldershot
Hampshire GU11 3HR
England

Ashgate Publishing Company
131 Main Street
Burlington, VT 05401-5600 USA

Ashgate website: http://www.ashgate.com

British Library Cataloguing in Publication Data
Assessing sociologists in higher education
  1.Sociology - Study and teaching (Higher) 2.Educational
  tests and measurements
  Harrison, Eric II.Mears, Robert
  301'.0711

Library of Congress Control Number: 2001089779

ISBN 0 7546 1645 2

Printed and bound by Athenaeum Press, Ltd.,
Gateshead, Tyne & Wear.

Contents

List of Tables and Figure

Tables

Figure

List of Contributors

John Abraham is Professor of Sociology at the University of Sussex.

Lee Barron is Lecturer in Sociology at the University of Northumbria at Newcastle.

Joan Chandler is Head of the Department of Sociology at the University of Plymouth.

Helen Graham is a Sociology graduate of the University of Sussex and is now working as manager of the Hanover Community Centre in Brighton.

Eric Harrison is a research student at Nuffield College, Oxford.

Barbara Harrison is Head of the Department of Sociology and Anthropology at the University of East London.

Alan Heslington works in the Quality Enhancement Unit at the University of Northumbria at Newcastle.

Victor Jupp is Head of the Sociology Division at the University of Northumbria at Newcastle.

Ruchira Leisten is Research Officer in the Centre for Research into Employment, Work and Training at University College, Northampton.

Robert Mears is Head of the Department of Sociology at Bath Spa University College.

Nod Miller is Professor in the Department of Innovation Studies and Assistant Vice Chancellor of the University of East London.

Andrew Pilkington is Head of the School of Social Studies at University College, Northampton.

Jennifer Platt is Professor of Sociology at the University of Sussex.

Tim Reed is a research student at the University of Sussex.

Rebecca Willison is at the Institute of Employment Studies, Sussex.

Chris Winch is Professor of Education at University College, Northampton.

Ruth Woodfield is Lecturer in Sociology at the University of Sussex.

Acknowledgements

Our initial debt must be to the one hundred or so sociologists who took part in some of the events and activities organised under the auspices of the *Assessment Strategies and Standards in Sociology* project. Without the participation and lively debates in workshops and meetings, this collection would be much the poorer.

We would like to acknowledge our gratitude to the Higher Education Funding Council of England and Northern Ireland, whose Fund for the Development of Teaching and Learning supported all the activities on which this book reports. However, we were only in a position to bid for the FDTL grant because of the success of sociologists at Bath Spa University College in the Teaching Quality Assessment exercise. Those colleagues at Bath Spa have been a source of support and inspiration before, during, and after the life of the project. Apart from their commitment to the discipline they also were unfailingly friendly and congenial.

'Keeping the show on the road' is of course the watchword of all time-limited projects and three project administrators ably assisted us in this during our two years. Helen Waterhouse got us off and running, treated us firmly but fairly, and made sure we had a programme of workshops to run. When Helen left for a Lectureship at the Open University, Nicky Wilson kindly saw us through the interim while also working for *History 2000*. Finally we were lucky enough to recruit Paulene Hudson, whose project management experience was essential in guiding us through the last frantic few months. She organised a great conference, and tolerated our shortcomings with good humour.

There are times when you wonder why you have ever started some things, and at those times it is important to have the support of staunch allies. For this we are indebted to the members of our steering committee and others working in the world of FDTL. However, special thanks are due to Sara Delamont for being such an effective Chairperson and advocate for our project. We would also like to thank Christine Eden, Chris Middleton and Clive Pearson for their friendship and camaraderie. From outside sociology we benefited hugely from getting to know Sally Brown and Phil Race. Graham Gibbs, from the Centre for Higher Education Practice at the

Open University, provided timely and useful interventions which kept the project on track, and us on our toes.

Above all, we would like to offer our thanks to the contributors to this book. At many times in the text we allude to the low status of pedagogic research in sociology. Given the limited funds and the onerous reporting requirements, there was very little incentive for them to get involved, but they responded with great skill and enthusiasm. Above all we thank them for their patience while we prepared the book for the publishers.

Eric Harrison and Robert Mears
Oxford and Bath

1 Introduction

ERIC HARRISON AND ROBERT MEARS

Introduction

Why write a book about assessment in sociology? During a period of rapid social change, surely there are more important things for sociologists to be doing than examining their own navels? After all, there is a world out there beyond our own practices and that is what we should be studying. This is a quite widespread view in the discipline. As we shall see in this book, sociologists tend not to regard the higher education system as worthy of analytical attention, least of all their own role and behaviour within that system. We do not share this view. This book takes its inspiration from Gouldner, Bourdieu and others who have been interested in constructing a 'sociology of sociology' (Reynolds and Reynolds, 1970). For us that means not just the way sociologists do their research, but the way they 'pass on' the discipline through their teaching (Goldsmid and Wilson, 1980), and the values they reward and reproduce through their assessment processes.

While our commitment in principle to this sort of sociology goes back some years, the immediate stimulus for this book was our professional involvement with the *Fund for the Development of Teaching And Learning* (FDTL). This initiative was launched by the HEFCE and DENI in December 1995 to support projects aimed at stimulating developments in teaching and learning and to encourage the dissemination of good practice across the higher education sector. This was to be achieved through subject-based networks or consortia.

Other initiatives had gone before it, most notably *Enterprise in Higher Education* (EHE) in the 1980s, and at the start of the 1990s the *Teaching More Students* project. FDTL was different however. For the first time the Council decided to promote change not through educational developers or continuing education units, but to make money available directly to practising academics for single discipline or inter-disciplinary activities. In common with many of our colleagues we had always espoused

1

our enthusiasm for teaching our subject. Now the funding council was putting its money where our mouths were.

In 1997 one of the editors (Mears) received a large grant under FDTL to fund a project called *Assessment Strategies and Standards in Sociology*. The other (Harrison) joined the team as the Project Officer at the start of 1998. For the next two years we immersed ourselves in issues that previously we had ignored or taken for granted. We gained an insight into the world of educational development. We attended conferences, we participated in workshops and we were advised and counselled on the best strategies for disseminating our ideas. In time we became educational developers ourselves, running our own workshops and seminars and offering input to smaller projects run by colleagues in our consortium. Having viewed teaching and assessment from sociology classrooms for a number of years, we now donned the spectacles of outsiders in our own discipline.

Whilst staff and educational developers had laboured in universities for years to try and raise the level of interest in teaching and learning issues, their success was limited. 'Generic' initiatives tended to flounder, as academics ignored exhortations to try something new or rethink existing teaching practices. It was all too easy for lecturers to dismiss generic activities with a response such as 'It may work for chemistry, but…'. This so-called 'not invented here syndrome' was an obstacle to the adoption of new ideas in teaching and learning. It seems obvious in retrospect that the decision to channel resources towards subject specialists, however inexperienced some of us were, was based on a realistic assessment of the limited achievements of conventional staff development. FDTL was based on the view that only sociologists (or chemists, lawyers etc.) could hope to have any impact on the classroom practices of other sociologists.

By the mid 1990s the demand to improve university teaching became pressing, partially because of the rapid expansion of student numbers and a more diverse student population. In addition there emerged more intrusive and public mechanisms for the evaluation of teaching quality. In other words there were growing internal and external pressures for university teaching quality to be taken more seriously than hitherto.

The first three chapters of this book examine the relationship between these twin forces for change, which we might term 'pressure from without' and 'pressure from within'. In chapter 2 Robert Mears places the FDTL initiative in the much wider context of higher levels of external regulation of universities and public concern about university standards. This chapter traces some of the developments that appear to challenge the autonomy of individual university teachers and the institutions in which they worked. Mears questions the failure of sociologists to locate their own experiences within broader sociological debates about the accountability of professions.

In chapter 3 Eric Harrison explores some of the debates about the purposes of teaching sociology. Drawing on American insights and some key contributions from British sociologists, he challenges us to take seriously some of the 'cultural contradictions' inherent in teaching the discipline. He notes the increasing convergence between the purposes of assessment and the purposes of the curriculum. The chapter also reports on the first ever survey of assessment practice in UK sociology departments. This focuses not just on the use of particular modes of assessment, but on more strategic issues to do with programme planning and peer review. It also reveals much about academic attitudes to the assessment process.

In chapter 4 Joan Chandler, a member of the QAA sociology benchmark panel, begins her discussion with an overview of the curriculum in fifteen 'excellent' sociology departments. This work was undertaken in an attempt to address questions about the nature of the discipline at undergraduate level. This is often depicted as 'fissiparous and fragmented'. Theoretical trends and moves towards inter-disciplinarity have undermined the belief in a disciplinary core. It may be surprising, therefore, that Chandler discovered strong similarities in the sociology curricula in departments with quite different institutional settings and missions. This made the task of subject benchmarking less controversial than it might initially appear. Chandler outlines three different approaches to benchmarking – minimal, promotional and developmental – and describes the strengths and weaknesses of each. The chapter concludes with a summary of the implications of these for the process of academic review in 2002.

The next four chapters describe the work of sociologists engaging in the practical attempts both to innovate and to improve more traditional assessment methods. Because the overview report (HEFCE, 1996) drew attention to the limited innovation in assessment in sociology departments, it was often assumed that we were the prophets of innovation. In fact we were suspicious of the idea that innovation is always desirable for its own sake and we were convinced that so-called traditional methods of assessment are valuable, but would benefit from a rethink. In other words, we were just as interested in encouraging sociologists to reflect upon existing dominant methods by which our students were assessed. This is why we were pleased that Pilkington and his colleagues agreed to develop a project on the sociology dissertation.

Chapter 5 points out that the dissertation, both in sociology and other cognate disciplines, occupies a semi-iconic status. It is widely felt among teachers that the dissertation exemplifies the integrative nature of the best sociology. Pilkington et al subject this tried and tested method to further scrutiny. They offer unsettling evidence of some unreliability of marking and argue that we need to reassure ourselves about marking standards in order to reassure others. A simplistic response to marker variability of this kind is to introduce more explicit criteria. Their research suggests that this apparent solution raises broader concerns about the balance of collegialism and managerialism in universities.

In chapter 6 Harrison and Miller offer some intriguing examples of some of the ways in which sociologists and other social scientists attempt to integrate biography and autobiography into student learning and assessment. They offer us a powerful rationale – the sociological imagination – for the kinds of work they describe and some tentative explanations of why such methods remain relatively underdeveloped. This is surprising in the context of an efflorescence of research interest in biography and autobiographical method. Why are the lived experiences of our students not more frequently harnessed in the interests of developing that much vaunted sociological imagination? They identify some possible reasons for this reluctance and offer some ways in which some of the potential problems might be addressed.

This general reluctance to innovate is echoed by Jupp and his colleagues in chapter 7. The impact of new technologies forms a vibrant area of research and discussion in sociology. It seems surprising, therefore, that sociologists have been slow to see the potential of computers for teaching, learning and assessment. The chapter reports in some detail on the efforts of one sociology department to develop tailor-made computer-assisted learning and assessment packages. It offers useful advice on this neglected area of innovation. It also addresses some of the commonly expressed objections – ranging from the epistemological to the practical. Jupp et al conclude that considerable efforts need to be directed towards developing high quality questions. If this is achieved, the evidence suggests that students will respond enthusiastically.

The involvement of students in assessment is also the theme of chapter 8. Educational developers have been urging academics to experiment by involving students in the assessment process. The claim is frequently made that this will motivate students and as a result will improve their understanding of assessment criteria and thereby their learning and their performance. The problem is that even 'explicit' criteria are often far from clear to students because they are not trained in the language in which those criteria are usually couched. Meanwhile, sociologists at Sussex had long been involving students in essay marking exercises. We gave them the opportunity to do this more systematically. Platt et al confronted a range of issues to do with measurement of performance and its interaction with authority relations. They constructed a quasi-experimental design from their established teaching practices. Using a mixture of observation, quantitative data and video material circulated to other departments, they gathered evidence about student marking behaviour. The strength of the chapter is its use of robust sociological methods to explore sociology teaching. The claimed benefits of innovative methods are subjected to the proper sociological response – 'show us the evidence'.

We conclude the book by attempting to draw some lessons from our experiences and those of our colleagues who participated in the consortium. Although the contributors were involved in quite disparate activities, their projects share certain principles. Firstly, they are operating within the context of sociology teaching but all draw, to some extent, on insights from colleagues in cognate disciplines. Secondly, they all treat the teaching of their subject as a reflective endeavour, informed by research. We argue that this 'scholarly' approach to teaching enhancement is the only one likely to earn legitimacy among colleagues. We strongly advocate the adoption of a scholarship of teaching and assessment within sociology and look ahead to the context in which this is most likely to take place.

Finally for this introductory chapter, we need to be clear about what this book is not. It does not aim to offer busy practitioners a few simple ideas for how they might adopt more innovative assessment methods. We have attempted that job elsewhere (Harrison and Mears, 2000). Instead we have encouraged our contributors to write about their practice from a sociological perspective. In doing so, we hope to have generated a specifically *sociological* response to the developing debate about assessment strategies and standards.

2 Called to Account: the Last Autonomous Profession

ROBERT MEARS

Introduction

Over the past decades UK universities have undergone major changes. There have been two significant periods of expansion. The Robbins Report of 1963 paved the way for the creation of new universities and polytechnics and a growing proportion of young people entering higher education. A second period of rapid growth occurred in the 1990s with the abolition of the binary divide and funding systems that encouraged increased student recruitment. Although the numbers of academics has not kept pace with the growth in student numbers, there have still been increased numbers and changes in the social characteristics of students and staff. This has led to some broadening of the social bases of academic life and a significant 'democratisation' of the academic profession (Halsey, 1992). In turn the changing student profile has called into doubt the effectiveness of some of the tried and tested means of teaching and assessing students.

There is little doubt that 'the social ambience of British Higher Education has changed. The older culture of higher learning and social exclusiveness persists but it sits alongside environments which differ greatly in architecture and temper' (Fenton et al, 2000). This shift from an elite to a mass system of higher education has brought with it new challenges for University teachers – not least of which is the pressure to rethink our teaching methods and the ways in which students learn. Some academic critics of university teaching claim that there is a growing gap between the routine practices of lecturers and the 'evidence-based' academic consensus about how to be better teachers. In addition, governments, students, employers and other 'stakeholders' demand more than ever from universities. No longer was it sufficient to certify graduates. Universities throughout the 1980s and 90s were encouraged to develop students' transferable skills, employability, enterprise and initiative, etc.

7

whilst teaching more of them. All this has taken place against a background of expansion, as well as funding and organisational reforms.

In addition universities began to experiment with modularisation, curriculum reform, more innovative types of assessment, and all in the context of an unprecedented level of external interest in what we do. As with all public services, universities faced the new challenge of 'accountability'. This included research and teaching and both were subjected to a degree of external evaluation that challenged traditional notions of academic freedom. Both of these core activities of Universities were subjected to systematic monitoring in the form of the Research Assessment Exercise (RAE) and Teaching Quality Assessment (TQA). The measurement of 'teaching quality', first by the HEFCE and subsequently by the QAA, brought a new transparency to the teaching activities of lecturers. In turn this led too much more emphasis on peer review of teaching within Departments. The TQA exercise also spawned a number of initiatives, of which the HEFCE Fund for the Development of Teaching and Learning (FDTL) is one. This aimed to improve University teaching through the identification and dissemination of good practice. Several of the key chapters in this collection report specific initiatives aimed at improving teaching and learning Sociology.

There has also been a major review of higher education conducted in 1997 by Lord Dearing (HMSO, 1997). One of the themes running through the Dearing Report was the need for Universities to invest in staff training and development to cope with the twin pressures of international competition in a globalising economy and the changing nature of employment. The Report advocated career-long continuous professional development and systematic disciplinary updating. Pennington argues that there are powerful reasons why continuous professional development of University teachers is essential in the context of 'the half-life of knowledge, the changing profile of students, the demands of lifelong learning and the potential of information technology' (Pennington, 2000: 7).

The changes occurring in the world of teaching and learning are also compelling lecturers to review the purpose and aims of previously taken for granted activities such as lectures and seminars (Gibbs, 1994). The learning outcomes movement urged lecturers to rethink the purposes and ways in which students were assessed. In particular there emerged a strong argument that assessment should be geared much more tightly to measuring what students could do as well as what they might know. There is also growing pressure for younger staff to gain accreditation for teaching either from some of the many in-house programmes offered to staff by Universities or from the newly established Institute for Learning and Teaching (ILT).

Working on the FDTL project raised a number of issues for us beyond the limited aims of 'disseminating good practice' in the teaching and learning of sociology. It was inevitable that as sociologists, we were drawn into much broader debates about the changing nature of the regulatory state and the role and place of sociology in making sense of these changes. It also raised a range of questions about the extent of central government 'interference' in academic life, the boundary between individual notions of academic freedom and the role of state agencies in regulating academic provision.

This thumbnail sketch of the challenges faced by Universities serves as an introduction to the main purpose of this chapter. I want to review briefly some of the ways in which the regulation of the teaching activities of academics has been achieved over the past twenty years. In addition I want to use our experience of working with teachers in sociology departments across England between 1998 and 2000 to speculate about responses to the 'quality' agenda. I also want to try to advance a tentative *sociological* explanation for new forms of regulation and surveillance. In other words, what can sociologists contribute to the debate about the apparent erosion of academic autonomy?

The Development of Regulation

A significant trend in UK social policy over the past two decades has been the attempt to reorganise public services so that they resemble in some ways the private sector. Universities, in common with the rest of the public sector, have been subjected to new regimes of managerialism, quasi-market mechanisms and attempts to change, not just the organisational forms, but also the occupational culture. An aspect of this process has been the attempt to subject public sector workers to novel ways of monitoring. Inspection and regulatory regimes have been introduced usually in the name of 'value for money' or 'quality'. This has been legitimised by the powerful rhetoric of consumerism and accountability. This rhetoric has frequently invoked the 'right' of the stakeholders in higher education – students, parents, and employers – to have access to more information to guide their decisions.

The various mechanisms by which accountability is achieved range from the relatively detached evidence of various performance indicators through to the more intrusive inspection visits (Hood et al, 2000). In public services in general, procedures have been introduced in which, 'standards are set, monitored and/or enforced in some way, by bureaucratic actors who are somewhat separate from units or bodies that have direct operational or service delivery responsibilities' (Hood and Scott, 1996: 321). The drive to refashion public services and the high prominence given to managerialism in that process is well documented (Rao, 1998). The new forms of managerialism in the Universities have involved systematic attempts to specify outcomes in more rigorous ways. I am not interested here in debating the merits or the validity of such measures. What is incontrovertible is that all public services, including Universities have been shifted away from measuring inputs towards the stipulation and refinement of outcomes. The terminology used to describe these processes – assessment, inspection, monitoring, audit – itself tells us something about the sensitivity of those being 'inspected' and reveals the extent of power differentials between different occupations. It is important to distinguish between inspection, with its connotations of explicit regulation, and various forms of assessment and research/advice (Hughes et al, 1998).

In retrospect it is possible to see the abolition of the binary divide and the creation of new Universities in 1992 as a watershed. At the time many saw the granting of the 'university' title to polytechnics and colleges as a reward for their achievements. With hindsight it is clear that, although there were possibilities for the 'new' Universities to compete in the RAE for sources of funding that had previously been denied to them, there were unanticipated consequences. A major consequence was the subjection of all universities to new centralised systems of funding and regulation. In other words, it represented a major way by which the chartered Universities could be brought under systems of 'quality' monitoring and evaluation.

The former Polytechnics, under the management of local authorities and accredited by the Council for National Academic Awards (CNAA) were accustomed to 'external' regulation. The creation of the HEFC and the QAA led to the public ranking of departments and Universities by research output and teaching quality. Such novel forms of intervention into the world of the traditional Universities undoubtedly led to opposition but with little apparent effect. The ranking of teaching quality also raised the issue of the relative status of research and teaching both for individuals, departments and Universities.

There is, of course, academic debate about the reasons for the rise of the 'audit culture' (Power, 1997). One general argument emphasises State efforts to control public spending in which most monitoring activities are Treasury-driven. Others claim that this is a political project aimed at strengthening the centralised state at the expense of local and regional centres of power and influence (Farnham and Horton, 1996). It is axiomatic that new styles of managerialism have gone hand in hand with more rigorous efforts to measure and assess the activities of service providers. The spread of performance indicators in Universities dates back to 1984.

The then Education Secretary, Sir Keith Joseph, announced that there would be a drive for greater efficiency in the Universities and performance indicators were a central part of this strategy. The claim was that performance indicators would guide policy making. This included 'selectivity in the distribution of resources, the rationalisation and where appropriate the closure of small departments, better financial management and *approved standards of teaching*' (Cave et al, 1988:25, my emphasis) (for a detailed example of performance indicators in higher education see Ashworth and Harvey, 1994). Writing more than a decade ago Cave and his associates comment, 'The use of PI's is a highly political issue. Their use, and the associated use of peer evaluation, which may be viewed as a form of PI, can be defined as the generation of judgements about performance and their transformation into managerial tools. They are being formally developed as part of an attempt to reorientate the higher education system towards more evaluation in general and more public forms of evaluation in particular' (Cave et al, 1988:17).

The creation of the funding councils was crucial to the aim of subjecting Universities to more direct government control (Scott, 1995). One of the obvious consequences of the activity of both the Funding Councils and the QAA was an erosion of institutional autonomy. As well as teaching quality assessment the QAA developed (and are currently developing!) codes of practice covering nearly every aspect of university activity. As *The Higher* commented, 'the number of new Quality Assurance Agency rules is set to top 200 as a total of 11 codes are published.... The total number of codes could reach 13, as two additional documents governing student information and student counselling are being considered' (Baty, 2001: 8). These codes are not simply about persuading HEI's to adopt 'best practice'. There are punitive consequences because 'failure to adhere to any of the precepts could lead to public criticism, and is ultimately linked to a university's public funding' (Baty, 2001: 8). It has been argued that up until the 1980s individual academics enjoyed a degree of autonomy and a 'strong sense of freehold which...have had few parallels in contemporary higher education' (Becher and Kogan, 1988: 155–6). By the turn of the century Universities operate under more external constraint than ever before, and all in the name of 'accountability'. Becher and Kogan claim that 'The subsequent extent of external intervention in both the structure and the processes of British higher education makes it impossible to sustain the earlier claims for an independent, self-determining network of institutions in which the basic unit reigns supreme' (1992, vi–vii). The days when a benign government handed 'grants' to the Universities Grants Committee to distribute among thirty or so Universities without any clear or open criteria has long gone. With the announcement in 2000 of the

HEFCE transparency review it seems as if all aspects of the life of the University academic – teaching research and administration – are open to ever deeper scrutiny (HEFCE, 2000).

While the issue of standards and quality – highly contested terms of course – were at the heart of the CNAA mission, there were few attempts to be explicit about the terms and their meanings. According to Silver (1990) 'A good deal of the CNAA's interest in questions of standards across the years has ...focussed both on attempts to clarify criteria and on...grappling with them in operation' (Silver 1990: 262). Traditionally the external examiner system was held up as the cornerstone of 'quality control' in the assessment and classification of students. Mass expansion surely killed off any lingering faith in this system. As concern about the quality of teaching and academic standards grew, bolstered by arguments about 'dumbing down', universities and their staff were obliged to respond to a new agenda about 'quality' articulated by external agencies.

In March 1998 the QAA welcomed the positive response of the Government to the Dearing report's proposals on the quality of University teaching. In a consultation exercise the QAA made clear that teaching quality would be guaranteed and improved by reviews of institutional systems. These systems must safeguard provision and regular reviews of subjects to, 'measure the outcomes they achieve against relevant threshold standards and the objectives specified for the programmes' (*Higher Quality*, Vol. 1, no. 3). What had once been an almost private activity between consenting adults was now open to scrutiny by peers and by external assessors. The revised QAA Academic Review of subjects beginning in 2001 assumes that all Universities will have in place systems of peer review and the monitoring of teaching quality. They will also seek evidence that data gathered through peer review is acted upon in ways that address the issue of teaching quality.

The post-Dearing agenda, driven by the Quality Assurance Agency has a number of aspects, to which all University teachers are required to respond. These include the elaboration and publication of programme specifications with associated learning outcomes; systems to ensure threshold standards via subject benchmarking; more interest in outcomes rather than classroom performance; improved student feedback and rigour and reliability in assessment. Some of this does entail a shift in the occupational culture of academics. No doubt the FDTL initiative was designed to address some of these issues.

When the history of higher education in the last decades of the twentieth century comes to be written, one of the questions that might exercise analysts is the limited extent of academic resistance to the mechanisms imposed to ensure 'accountability'. Whilst the pages of *The*

Higher yields examples of individual complaints against the burdens placed on lecturers and on institutions, the surprising thing is the relatively muted response of academics to the systems that have emerged over the past decade. It may be that academics decided that railing against such processes was politically naïve and pragmatism won the day.

The justification for this encroachment on the autonomy of universities took many forms. The familiar charge made by neo-liberals was that State-funded universities enjoyed a monopoly, which led to inefficiency and a lack of responsiveness to consumer demand. The neo-liberal right argued that professionally dominated services were relatively impervious to consumer criticism. The benefits of monopoly granted professionals immunity to public criticism because there was usually no alternative to existing provision. As part of a more general attack on public provision, the new right regarded professionalism as a device to protect elite occupations from the bracing effects of market forces. It is misleading to link a more critical approach to public sector professionals as the prerogative of the new right. Before the 'Thatcherite onslaught' influential analyses from the left had also encouraged a more critical perspective on professional power (see Clarke et al, 1994). Sociologists were, after all often at the forefront of developing critical analyses of professional dominance. Sociologists were particularly scornful of the self-aggrandising claims of powerful professions and attacked medics, for example, for the limited nature of professional accountability (Stacey, 1992).

A powerful defence of academic autonomy is essential when it comes to research and scholarship. Becher and Kogan spell out why good intellectual work, in whatever subject, must be supported because, 'the closer the work is to the frontiers of knowledge, the fewer there are in a position to assess it. So, it must follow the academic world as a whole has in many such cases to be trusted to certify the quality of the activities in which it is engaged. Therein lies the strength of the twin academic traditions of autonomy and a highly competitive environment. For the most part work of quality cannot be done under control from above' (Becher and Kogan, 1992: 188). Whilst this may legitimise research freedom, in which only a small number of peers may be in any position to judge, this requires trust. The cry of 'protect academic freedom' is much less convincing when extended to teaching, learning, curriculum and assessment.

As Becher and Kogan comment, 'The classic and autonomous ideal of the government of higher education is one which has never been fully realised in any but a few prestigious universities, let alone in the whole range of British higher education institutions' (Becher and Kogan, 1992: 177). Highly prized by academics even if it only ever existed in some idealised form and for a few elite and prestigious universities before mass expansion, 'higher education failed to convince government of its undisputed claim to do good by doing what academics wanted to' (ibid: 179). Consequently, the days when Universities were virtually free to set their own objectives and create their own programmes of research, scholarship and teaching are rapidly disappearing.

The Inspection and Enhancement of University Sociology

The 1995/6 TQA visits to 76 English sociology departments concluded that 99 per cent of observed teaching sessions were 'excellent' or 'very good'. The Overview Report (HEFCE, 1996) noted that use was made of a wide range of teaching and learning methods. The Report concluded that, 'the best classroom sessions were well organised and involved a stimulating presentation where lecturers current research findings focussed on analysis and interpretation rather than on the presentation of factual material. The lecturers engaged the students and encouraged them to think, question and reflect. Given clear direction, students knew that they would be expected to have read the set materials and successful outcomes were achieved...The main characteristics found in the best teaching sessions were the establishment of clear objectives and the content placed within an appropriate framework which was shared with the students. Such criteria are mentioned in some 80 per cent of the reports'.

Despite this clean bill of health from the first ever systematic review of sociology teaching nationally, the pressure for further training for University teachers and greater innovation in curriculum delivery and assessment continues. Changes in the organisation and funding of higher education have necessitated considerable innovation in the delivery of Sociology courses. This 'Copernican shift' away from an emphasis on teaching and lecturer performance to the whole process by which students learn, is widely accepted by sociologists – at least at the level of rhetoric. Most sociologists are keen to embrace an image of the student as an active learner and the process of learning as a co–operative venture involving high levels of transparency about aims, outcomes and assessment. In reality, of course, inertia, organisational priorities and aspects of the occupational culture of University teachers may militate against change. The broader challenge to university teachers has come from a disparate range of interests; the State (in its demand for 'value for money'); an enlarged and more diverse student population; business and employer interests who have argued, with some success that Universities are failing to prepare students adequately for the labour market.

It would be extraordinary if such fundamental changes in the Universities did not lead to some resistance. This has taken several forms. University Vice-Chancellors have used the consultation process with the QAA to renegotiate the detail of draft proposals. Sometimes this has resulted in partial victories for the Universities on issues such as the right to choose external examiners. At the 'grass roots' university teachers have grumbled about the burden of RAE and TQA but when it came to the crunch there was compliance. The benchmarking initiatives were also greeted with mistrust because they were seen by many as an embryonic national curriculum for higher education. There is also widespread scepticism about the attempts to construct programme specifications and detailed learning outcomes. Power (1997) refers to situations where staff simply go through the motions as ritualistic compliance. Further research is needed to test the extent to which staff have presented a façade of compliance when faced with the requirements of regulation.

Subordinating academics to novel forms of surveillance and regulation represented a major structural and ideological shift because, despite the occasional critical voice, assessment of the performance of lecturers was viewed as unnecessary. The benign view was that regulation and monitoring in the name of quality was redundant. The specific values and norms of academic life – a service orientation, vocationalism even – guaranteed commitment to 'quality' performance. Others argued that the measurement of performance was somehow too difficult, that the process of learning, involving some mystical transference of insight and understanding between initiate and novice was not amenable to any straightforward measurement. In a parody of Bagehot's views on the British monarchy, arguments were advanced at FDTL workshops against the specification of learning outcomes because this would undermine the mystery of higher education. The process of learning, involving the transmission of knowledge and insight, would be destroyed if light was to be cast on it. In private discussions, sociologists have argued that attempts to measure the achievement of specified 'outcomes' are actually counter to 'good education'. In practice, critics of accountability initiatives conflated methodological and principled objections.

Of course those sociologists who worked on FDTL projects had many reservations about a simple model which purported to identify excellence and then disseminate examples of 'best practice'. Academic cultures are inimical to such straightforward notions of dissemination. In the course of our work on the project on assessment and standards the indifference, and sometimes outright opposition of sociologists to 'external interference' in the work of departments was a leitmotif. Although we cannot claim to have systematic data about the reaction of sociologists to these various initiatives, we encountered considerable indifference or even opposition to initiatives aimed at addressing teaching and learning issues.

It is to be expected that individual academics will have preferences about the balance of their work as researchers and or teachers and about the mode and style of teaching and learning in which they engage. As the education development literature testifies, shifting individual teaching styles is not easy. It has been argued that the 'exhortation to teach better – or to facilitate better learning – will have little impact unless departmental cultures are conducive to better teaching. Likewise, attempts to improve teaching by coercion run the risk of producing compliance cultures…while simultaneously compounding negative feelings about academic work' (Knight and Trowler, 2000: 69).

The transformation of universities has certainly undermined some aspects of collegial working. For example, what we termed a 'strategic' approach to assessment depends, in part, on whole departments meeting together to review student assignments. The days when time was set aside to pore over colleagues' exam papers or essay questions are disappearing. (see p. 33 in this volume). For understandable reasons – the pressure to publish, rising student numbers, administrative burdens – it has been suggested that, 'The opportunity to share and discuss good practice and problems in teaching and learning is increasingly lost' (Knight and Trowler, 2000: 72). Our work in Sociology Departments tends to confirm this.

This tells us something about the relative status accorded to undergraduate teaching relative to the production of research output (see Harrison in this volume). Several of the participants at FDTL workshops argued that it was impossible to understand such apparently benign initiatives without connecting them to the larger picture of increasing regulation or 'interference' in the life of Universities. We were accused of naivety for not realising that the FDTL projects were a mere 'cover' for State efforts to reduce expenditure on University teaching. We were told that the whole FDTL initiative was a cynical exercise aimed at diverting attention away from the declining unit of resources in Universities. Opposition from some of the more prestigious sociology departments to the whole process of subject benchmarking is further evidence of cynicism about the involvement of state agencies in specifying the detail of the curriculum.

Despite the widespread cynicism amongst academics, what is significant about the emerging regulatory frameworks of higher education is the role being given to academics as participants in the process – either as teaching quality assessors, members of research assessment panels, benchmark panels and academic reviewers and auditors. The QAA has sought to involve subject associations in an attempt to improve its legitimacy amongst academics. In fact, the composition of the QAA benchmark panel was based on nominations from the British Sociological Association (see Chandler in this volume). The creation of the Quality Assurance Agency signalled a change from earlier forms of quality assurance.

Kogan (1988) differentiates between three types of accountability to which higher education has been subjected. He identifies 'the public contractual and managerial mode... the professional mode in which the academic collegial and hierarchies operate; and the consumerist modes of accountability in which different proxies for a market are present' (1988: 169). These are often contradictory and imply different modes of regulation and accountability. The current situation with UK higher education involves an uncomfortable mixture of all of these.

The demand for greater accountability can also be seen as an integral component of democratic discourses. The spread of a more egalitarian ethos may well underpin the demand for the performance of public servants to be made more open to scrutiny. A belief in meritocracy bolsters demands for professionals, including academics, to be made more accountable. The language of citizenship can also play an important part in legitimising the 'right' of 'stakeholders' to have more information about what it is that Universities do and what is involved in subject knowledge. The activities of the twenty six QAA subject benchmark panels in specifying the nature of the subject is justified in terms of explicit criteria for comparing the standards of courses but also for enabling new constituencies of parents and potential students to make informed choices about subjects and institutions. Again the move from an elite to a mass system is crucial in making sense of these processes.

The Last Autonomous Profession?

Sociologists can learn a great deal about the contested nature of 'quality' by looking at developments in other public services. The recent period has seen an unprecedented public debate about medical dominance and the lack of accountability of the medical profession. Debates on 'quality' in the NHS have become conflated with a more general concern with accountability. The new managerialism in the NHS demanded more information about the relationship between inputs and outcomes, and this inevitably involved a greater degree of scrutiny of professional actions than had ever occurred before. The whole tenor of the debate about the medical profession and health policy has changed in recent years. Previously there were a host of critical studies which emphasised the autonomy of the profession, their closed and self-regarding activities, the absence of effective complaints procedures, the limited influence of consumers on medical practice and the fact that most routine medical procedures were conducted without reference to evaluation, effectiveness, patient approval etc. The intriguing thing about this process is the initial reluctance of the medical profession to be involved in studies of 'quality', followed by enthusiastic embrace.

Once collegial forms of regulation are undermined or discredited then relations based purely on traditional notions of trust become untenable. In its place are more explicit systems of review. Klein refers to this as a shift from 'status' to 'contract'. Referring to the medical profession, Klein suggests that 'The concordat between State and profession is, in a sense, being renegotiated...the days of self-regulated autonomy may be drawing to a close' (Klein, 1990: 130). Moving towards public and explicit regulation and accountability is an example of this shift from 'status' to 'contract'. Trusted occupations that once relied on their taken for granted authority are increasingly compelled to demonstrate their ability to meet performance targets. As the performance of teachers, academics, doctors and the like becomes open to scrutiny we see the relentless logic of Weberian rationality at work. What is surprising is not that academics are being subjected to such scrutiny but that it took so long.

The 'decline of donnish dominion' can be seen in sociological terms as part of a more general decline of status and trust in established professions and traditional institutions. The 'detraditionalisation' processes of late modernity operate to undermine any straightforward trust in institutions such as Universities. At a societal level, the decline of deference and the claim that late modernity has ushered in an era of greater scepticism regarding expert knowledge must surely be implicated (Giddens, 1992). Even without the neo-liberal assault on public services, critical questions about the performance of public sector professionals have been asked in the last decade. The decline in deference goes along with the shift from relations based on trust and status to those based more explicitly on contractual relations (Klein, 1990). For Klein, the concept of status 'involves...a particular view of society which sees it as being composed of corporations or guilds that in turn confer status and authority on their members. Such bodies have leased out to them the powers of the state. They regulate their members, enjoy a high degree of autonomy and judgement of competence is made by members of the guild, that is professional peers; lastly but importantly, they operate on trust' (1990: 127). In contrast, systems based on contractual relations place much more emphasis, 'on public regulation, not on the role of peers but that of hierarchy, not on trust but on review' (Klein, 1990: 128). The changes sketched in this chapter, in particular the increasing role of regulatory agencies such as QAA in the life of universities, seem to fit with Klein's analysis.

This is not the place to review the substantial body of sociological work on professional power and social closure. What can be discerned from the sociological literature is a strongly iconoclastic approach with regard to professional claims. Our own professional association, the BSA, grappled for years with issues about exclusivity and closure and the proper role of a professional body in maintaining 'standards'. What is clear is that sociologists have been by and large sceptical of occupational claims to be 'special' and more interested in the ways in which the division of labour is constructed and policed. Sociologists have tended to view professional self-beliefs as self-aggrandising and or self-seeking. (For a useful review of sociological approaches to professional power see Saks, 1990.) Consequently we find ourselves in a relatively weak situation when the profession seeks to guarantee standards of sociological curriculum and teaching by opposing external interference.

There are apparently paradoxical trends emerging. On the one hand levels of professional resistance to the accountability and 'quality' agendas seems to be waning. This may be because, as Pilkington et al suggest in this volume, academics are getting involved in 'regulatory' activities in order to pre-empt interference by 'outsiders'. Academics who agreed to serve on national Benchmark panels did so sometimes reluctantly but were motivated by a wish to avoid the imposition of more draconian monitoring regimes. As more people are actually involved in the accountability process, younger staff may enjoy career enhancement if they can show they are keen participants in the process. Careers can now be carved in the world of the *qualitocracy*.

Conclusion

The drive to make public sector professionals more 'accountable' is not a matter of party politics. Whichever party forms the government, it will ensure that, 'both the market and the strengthening of management objectives will more confidently challenge the power of the professional academic at the base of the system' (Becher and Kogan, 1992: 176). Anyone who seriously believes that the next decades will see an efflorescence of individual autonomy is surely mistaken. Sociologists might be in a strong position to help to shape the agenda of teaching and learning in ways that protect what we see as the core of our discipline. I would argue then that the drive for 'quality' can be appropriated and even transformed into something far removed from the intentions of managerialists.

Among the questions that we need to address is the extent to which sociologists can engage in a version of 'regulatory capture'. We can learn from other occupations in the ways in which the more distasteful aspects of external regulation have been renegotiated. In some cases public service providers are able to redefine or even resist external accountability. Sociologists ought to be in a strong position to draw upon our theories to make sense of these changes. In common with other public sector professionals, University teachers face a struggle to retain some of the traditional aspects of autonomy but within a framework of accountability that is probably inescapable. We have witnessed in universities a move away from trust in individuals to a more overarching trust in institutional mechanisms of accountability.

3 The Practice of Assessing Sociology

ERIC HARRISON

Introduction

This chapter focuses on the enhancement of the assessment process from within the sociology community rather than from outside through public regulation. It is organised into two main sections. The first reflects on the fact there has been so little interest in assessment issues among sociologists. It argues that this results from the ambiguous status of university teaching, an underdeveloped disciplinary infrastructure in comparison with longer-established subjects, and an uneasy relationship between sociology and the whole notion of 'professional closure'. The second section reports the findings of a survey of assessment practice in sociology conducted as part of the *Assessment Strategies and Standards in Sociology* project. The results offer a partial picture of the way British sociologists are approaching these problems, but they also raise a great many questions to which we have only speculative answers.

Sociology, Teaching and Professionalism

At the outset of our FDTL projects it quickly became apparent that the whole notion of the way the discipline should be assessed was a non-issue for discussion in British sociology. There are a number of reasons why this might be so, and the first of these is relatively straightforward. Assessment is a form of teaching activity and in the last decade two developments have combined to undermine the status of teaching. The principal change has been the increased selectivity of research funding and its linkage to measures of research output, through the Research Assessment Exercise (RAE). The second, though often overlooked, is the awarding of the University title to the former polytechnics and their entry into the

21

competition for research funding. As a result there has been a certain convergence of mission in the sector as 'new universities' scented a chance to grab funding from somewhat complacent older institutions. The latter have responded ferociously to this challenge by reorganising departments, engineering early retirements and creating new swathes of 'research lectureships'.

This convergence in terms of research-orientation has not been matched by a corresponding interest in the teaching of the subject to undergraduates. While the American Sociological Association has a permanent section devoted to the teaching of undergraduates and a dedicated journal *Teaching Sociology*, the British response has been much more sporadic and limited in scope. Partly perhaps in response to the intensification of teaching workloads and widespread unease about the effects of unsuitable accommodation, inadequate libraries, and dubious entry standards on the quality of teaching, many academics have sought a retreat in their research activity. At the same time the abolition of the binary divide has removed a status distinction from within the discipline. No doubt many academics have used the emphasis on research over teaching as a way of differentiating themselves from colleagues in the 'degree factories' that were the old Polytechnic sector. Equally, academics in post-1992 Universities have been eager to emulate the research-orientation of their opposite numbers in the older institutions. At a professional level there is something deeply rational about this behaviour. Teaching has become massified, with inadequate time or opportunity to form bonds with individual students. Many large courses are of necessity taught in more tightly structured and pre-specified packages, with institutions keen to ensure consistency of student experience. The perceived loss of autonomy and the mild Taylorism of the mass system results in a drop in the status ascribed to the activity of teaching. More means worse. The only escape routes are to institutions with more generous staff-student ratios (increasingly few) or into a research orientation that allows one to minimise contact with undergraduates.

There are strong incentives for individuals to decide to substitute research for teaching in response to the changing reward system. It is also clear that this has taken place at institutional level as newer universities, traditionally committed to the teaching function, have broadened their aspirations and suffered from mission creep as a result. In the case of sociology it has also taken place at the level of the subject association. For much of the 1970s and 1980s the discipline was concerned with defending its access to research council funding and arguing the case for preserving a social science research base. As we shall see the issue of the undergraduate curriculum was raised in the 1980s but never effectively institutionalised.

The content of the top journals has become much more 'research' oriented; there are fewer topic overviews, literature reviews or trend reports, and rarely if ever a piece dealing with the teaching of the subject. The Research Assessment Exercise has effectively reclassified much work not submitted as 7,000 word articles to peer reviewed journals as 'not research' and publishers frequently complain that they cannot find authors willing to write books for undergraduate audiences. When the BSA revamped its committee structure in 1998, it excluded any organ to deal with undergraduate matters. A Teaching and Learning Committee was only set up following the Annual Conference of that year in response to lobbying from a small section of academics involved in developmental projects. If Sociology is still a vocation in the 1990s it is now presented in terms of a research culture.

What is remarkable is that although research activity is the dominant discourse of the discipline it does not accurately reflect the main function of academic sociology. Even at the start of the twenty-first century nine tenths of the average department's budget will come from central government in return for educating undergraduates. This is the bread and butter of most academics and sociologists are no different. Perkin (1969) argued that Oxford and Cambridge grew in response to the needs of the Church and society. 'The medieval university was thus concerned entirely with professional education. The students, undergraduate and postgraduate, were in process of acquiring, first, a licence to teach and, second, a licence to practise law, medicine or theology' (Perkin, 1969: 9–10). Undergraduate numbers shrank from the sixteenth century onwards and universities became detached, self-perpetuating oligarchies. Perkin argues therefore that 'the rise of a modern profession of university teaching in the nineteenth century, though a revolution in itself, was therefore a revival rather than a departure, a rebirth rather than a genesis, a resurrection rather than a new creation' (Perkin 1969: 14).

This reminds us that the whole notion of a 'discipline' is based on the assumption of an extended training in the service of improvement; it is a branch of learning or instruction. While research and teaching have been regarded as indispensable to one another, at a structural level disciplines must be transmitted as disciplines if they are to survive as such. As one reviewer of sociology textbooks recently argued:

> Sociology, like all academic disciplines, is not just formally constituted by the sum of its research and current debates about scholarship, by its formal intellectual life. It is actively constructed in higher education institutions by its apprentices who are learning its style as well as its content. Introductory texts are very powerful

instruments for the creation of a sociology canon, a disciplinary 'character' and an intellectual culture (Bailey, 1998: 203).

The ongoing contradiction between the 'cutting edge' and the classroom has also been addressed in an American context:

> First, the largest and most enduring audience for sociology is undergraduate students. They are the chief source of employment for the profession. Yet there is an ambivalent relationship between sociologists and those who come to hear their message... We need the students to survive, but they offer negligible opportunities for professional advancement and often are a source of embarrassment for the profession... When we reflect on our largest perennial audience, we acknowledge our need for undergraduate students, but too often, they bring neither intellectual stimulation to individual sociologists nor academic acclaim to the profession (Baker and Rau, 1990: 169).

What they term this tension 'between dependency and embarrassment' relates to a second problem, which is the poor fit between undergraduate and graduate training in sociology. In contrast to the rigour of postgraduate courses, the undergraduate curriculum has 'so many thinly constructed courses that minimise intellectual achievement or critical reasoning...' (ibid: 169). Such remarks seem to echo UK critics of the drift to modularity and the alleged 'dumbing down' of undergraduate degrees. In addition they argue that throughout the 1960s sociology enjoyed rising undergraduate numbers because it was perceived by prospective applicants as the subject which would prepare them for 'working with people' or more specifically for posts in the social services, social welfare and criminal justice. At the same time academic sociology was working hard to disabuse students of this notion and distancing itself from such vocationalism. 'The 1960s can be described as the decade in which sociology continued to advance its cultural purity and unwittingly became further alienated from its undergraduate students constituency' (ibid: 172).

Baker and Rau move on to map the subsequent fracturing and specialisation of the discipline, tracing critiques from within such as Gouldner (1971) and concluding that this presents enormous difficulties for those charged with delivering the undergraduate curriculum. In retrospect they argue, the sociology curriculum has always been a very loose entity comprising a theoretical legacy (classical nineteenth and twentieth century social theory), a methodological legacy (based on the social survey as a tool but incorporating developments in qualitative fieldwork) and what they term 'the civic legacy of substantive topics' many of which rely on contributions from other fields but frequently become identified as 'sociological' (family, crime, race etc.). Their critique of undergraduate courses concerns both content (what we teach) and the skills of the teaching-learning process (how we teach) and generates a series of ideal-type approaches to curriculum ('high culture', 'civic sociology of the well informed citizen', 'watered down sociology', 'pop sociology'). Which of these might be adopted is seen to be contingent upon the needs of the audience, i.e. whether they are on a single honours programme, majors or non-majors (ibid: 184). In essence the style and content should be in harmony with the overall aims of the course.

Rethinking the Curriculum: what is Sociology *for* these days?

If we accept Baker and Rau's assumption that what constitutes a sociology curriculum is to some extent contingent upon what its purpose is, then we are led to ask the crucial question 'what is a degree in sociology for'? In his 1986 Presidential address, Martin Albrow made the point that if the main purpose of sociology departments was 'the furtherance of the discipline' then one could probably justify three large departments. This still left the vast bulk of the 78 providers in Britain without an apparent rationale. Albrow was keen to debunk what he calls the 'Myth of Heroic Struggle', an idea that the discipline had fought against an establishment conspiracy and against the odds had triumphed. Rather, he argued, sociology had been welcomed and proved popular primarily as a broad educational experience.

> Our degree courses have developed not to supply a small requirement for academic or publicly employed sociologists but, above all, to meet the continuing demands of the sociological movement, the mass of people who have opted to study sociology for their intellectual and personal betterment and those employers who understand that sociology may provide a highly suitable education preparatory to work (Albrow, 1986: 339).

In other words there are at least three groups of potential customers for our product: apprentice academic sociologists; those who plan to use the degree to enter the state bureaucracy in some capacity, who we might call professional sociologists (and see Albrow, 1970); and the 'well informed citizen' to adapt Baker and Rau's typology which was touched on earlier in this discussion. This was also a common theme during the expansion of the university system during the 1960s. The inaugural lectures of two Heads of the famous Leicester department both concerned themselves explicitly with such issues (see Neustadt, 1964 and Banks, 1971). Albrow draws on his experience of drafting syllabi for 16 and 18 year olds for the Welsh Joint Education Committee and contrasts the informed and reflexive curriculum discussions in which he was involved with its absence in HE. 'It is something of a paradox', he remarks, 'that the nature of our subject makes its extent so open to negotiation and yet, with the exception of teaching gender, the curriculum has been recently so little contested' (Albrow 1986: 432).

At the heart of the TQA methodology was the philosophy that no single yardstick could be used to measure every institution. The sector was now so diverse in terms of mission and organisation, and a discipline like sociology was so notoriously contested as to have virtually no common ground. The best the bureaucracy could do was judge how well each department or subject group was meeting its own aims. Anyone reading about the fragmentation of the discipline and the emergence of new paradigms would have expected the exercise to reveal little evidence of a common undergraduate curriculum. In deference to the specificity of 'academic tribes' (Becher 1989, 1994) the assessors were drawn from a large pool of 96 practising sociologists.

The results of the overall subject review could be regarded as surprising by some. Instead of the fissiparous and fragmented discipline of common mythology, there appeared a subject that was increasingly convergent across the sector. Many of the findings echoed the results of the earlier short-lived BSA Degree Curriculum Sub-Committee (e.g. Gubbay, 1993). Essentially the assessors had regarded an adequate diet of theory and methods to be indispensable. Individual reports call for greater elements of classical theory or exposure to a broader range of methodological approaches. Not only was there considerable consensus as to content, but also there emerged quite a consistent line on the use of mixed modes of assessment. Many reports call for final year students to be required to complete an extended piece of independent writing (a project or dissertation) in order to achieve an honours degree. Taken together, the 76 written reports on sociology provision and the summaries of aims and objectives stand as the most up-to-date and comprehensive record we have of the undergraduate curriculum in sociology. It is extraordinary that it took an external regulatory initiative to produce this information, even though it was sociologists as assessors who did the uncovering. As Stina Lyon has pointed out 'it seems a shame that it took a year of such tense and time consuming hard work for such prima facie simple and sensible conclusions to be reached' (Lyon, 1998: 10).

It may be far from obvious that a concern with the subject curriculum necessitates an interest in assessment practice. Until recently this was also true in mainstream education. Broadfoot observes that '[W]hilst its Siamese twin, curriculum, dominates bookshelves, professional training, and research and development work, the study of assessment has been confined largely to that of techniques' (Broadfoot, 1990: 649). However it has become increasingly recognised that if a curriculum consists not only of content but what are generically (and often somewhat sniffily) referred to as 'skills elements', then assessment regimes have not only to access a sample of candidates' knowledge but somehow test their ability to practice. Payne (1998) makes this point forcibly in the context of sociology:

> While being able to read, understand and critique other sociologists' work is a major requirement of being a sociologist, sociology also exists as *practice*. Doing sociology entails more than a passive sociological imagination; not least examining evidence, constructing new ideas, and creating new meanings. The practice of sociology, at its best, involves social skills like negotiation, listening, co-operating and empathising, and technical skills in information retrieval and effective presentation (Payne, 1998: 5).

Broadfoot argues that educationalists have come to see assessment as an integral part of a scheme of work and recognised its motivational role in the development of learning. In an attempt to give voice to this new and 'inextricable' bond between the two she coined the term 'curssessment' (Broadfoot, 1990: 653). It seems likely that some of the experiments described elsewhere in this volume are results of this merger, or certainly imply the need to apply it to the provision of undergraduate sociology.

The Significance of Disciplinary Differences

Albrow argued a decade ago that sociologists had been strangely mute about the practice of teaching their own discipline. This is still the case at the start of the new century. I have already examined some reasons why this should be so relative to research, but even more notable is the comparison with other cognate disciplines. I mentioned earlier the relatively active American approach to teaching issues; it is also true that other disciplines in the British system have engaged more with the problem of teaching. Psychology stands as a particularly interesting case, given that the study of how people learn is a core element of any psychology curriculum. Many educational development professionals have backgrounds in the subject, and most research on teaching and learning in HE relies on concepts imported from psychology.

Brown (1997) recently reviewed the main literature on student learning. More particularly he documented the effects that assessment strategies have on learning, but also noted the effects of departmental cultures. He recalls Argyris's distinction between 'espoused theories' and 'theories in use' when it comes to looking at how a department approaches its course design, management and assessment. It was this distinction, the lack of fit between the stated educational aims and day-to-day practice, which was commented on frequently by TQA assessors and in many cases led to the docking of points. For instance academics would claim to be developing in students methodological and other presentational skills that they claimed would be of vocational use. On closer inspection however it became difficult to see just how and where these were ever achieved in the undergraduate curriculum. Brown concludes his review with a call for research on teaching to hold equal weight in psychology with other research, on the grounds that firstly every subject has an implicit pedagogy that needs explicating, and secondly psychology has a special claim in this area because 'learning, teaching and assessment are part of the very stuff of psychology' (1997: 122).

Radford's (1997) overview starts from a different perspective, considering academic psychologists in terms of four models; parasites (echoes here of Urry's (1981) depiction of sociology), priests, proletariat and professionals. He favours the further development of the last model, which implies self-regulation, qualification and responsibility. The development of the British Psychological Society has long been regarded as a case study contrasting with the more open practice of the BSA. A key feature of a profession is of course a monopoly over knowledge and in many cases this involves the setting of a fixed curriculum or at least a common core which guarantees 'fitness to practice' as it were.

Geography is another discipline which has been far more advanced in considering these issues. Indeed there has been an extensive debate amongst academic Geographers about the core elements of the undergraduate curriculum. In reviewing the arguments Bradford (1995) though opposing the development of such a common core, recognises the arguments for doing so in a mass system of HE. Firstly that it is a natural progression from secondary education; such a standardisation could be sued to compare institutions, increase competition and drive up standards. Secondly such a standardisation has already taken place at the higher level of postgraduate training. Concern about the quality of doctoral training in the social sciences led to a review of many aspects of that practice (Burgess, 1994) and the outcome has been more prescriptive research training elements in PhD programmes, especially those that continue to be recognised by ESRC. Both Johnston (1997) and Unwin (1997) have opposed the idea of a core curriculum, the former on the grounds that 'geography is an academic discipline not a profession' and involved education not training. Unwin has six objections: 1) a core would become stagnant and at odds with the idea of a university, 2) knowledge should remain flexible to be emancipatory, 3) smaller departments would lack the ability to teach right across a common core, 4) the core is the least exciting area of the discipline and would reduce the attractiveness of the subject to students in the marketplace, 5) a core might well be imposed by blinkered individuals outside the discipline and 6) the subject would become a subservient provider of technical knowledge for the capitalist system.

Whatever the eventual outcome of these many debates, what is striking is the intellectual quality of the discussion in Geography. It is this sort of scholarly approach to teaching, learning and assessment which has, to the best of my knowledge, been lacking from sociology and needs to take place more publicly (a welcome exception to this being the recent exchange between Parker and Mouzelis (1997), in terms of content if not tone). Part of the reason this has not done so is the reluctance of sociologists to organise in the style of a professionally closed grouping.

I noted earlier that American sociology has long been a more professionally organised operation than in the UK. Even back in the 1960s Inkeles remarked that 'Sociology is not only an intellectual discipline, it is also a profession' (1964: 106). Janowitz went further in so far as he identified it as implicitly a teaching-centred profession. 'As an academic profession, students are, of course, the immediate clients of sociologists. It is a professed goal that the academic sociologist will accept the responsibility to teach, although the audience for teaching may be variously defined to include other professional groups or extra-mural assemblies' (Janowitz, 1972: 105). There is an argument that sociology in Britain was at its inception much more concerned with teaching matters than now. In a preliminary comment on her forthcoming history of the association, Platt (1997) observes that 'professionalism' has been a recurring idea over its fifty-year life. Ironically a key issue in the 1950s and 60s was that of who should count as a sociologist.

> The younger generation, with formal qualifications in sociology, naturally wanted those to count for something, and were anxious about job opportunities. The older establishment was concerned to keep the Association's activities accessible to the majority wider membership, and did not want to cater for specialist subgroups. It was in response to this that the 'Teachers' Section', formed in the early 1960s, opened a new period. The TS was not exclusive to university teachers of sociology, but entry was only allowed through gates specifying professional qualifications. There was a real concern with teaching issues... but that was not its only activity... it organised the first summer school, and it initiated *Sociology* [the journal] (Platt 1997: 2–3).

Ironically the TS was later disbanded as the subject expanded and splintered into a series of research study groups. However Platt argues that in one form or another, 'professionalism' has been a recurring idea during the association's history, and it seems safe to predict that it will continue to do so for the foreseeable future. It is ironic that during the 1960s it was an involvement in teaching that defined a sociologist as a high status member of the profession. That process went sharply into reverse in the 1990s.

The Practice of Assessment

Whether or not the relative status of the teaching function within sociological practice is wholly to blame for the lack of innovation in assessment, the fact remains that the result of the 1995/96 round of inspections was a clear indication that in around half of departments there was no variety outside the established trinity of the unseen examination, the coursework essay, and the project/dissertation. This said, these are merely vehicles for the delivery of student assessment. Even within this threefold framework there is an enormous range of styles of task or question possible.

A key question for the project was to make a preliminary exploration of the way assessment practice had changed since the inspectors' visits. While our primary aim was simply to establish a descriptive account we had at the back of our minds the possible effects of two separate but related stimuli. Firstly, of course there was the effect of the TQA process and the legacy of the reports it left behind at institutional and subject levels. It seemed reasonable to expect that, regardless of any ideological commitment to greater diversity, academics might find themselves under pressure from their own management to innovate. Secondly, however, we had to consider our own project activities as an additional 'independent variable' (although strictly speaking our existence was itself the outcome of the report and was therefore secondary to it). We had visited many of the departments in England, and colleagues from at least two dozen departments contributed through our workshops. Taken as a whole the project had encompassed nearly forty departments through one event or another. Our mailings as part of the SSP2000 umbrella had reached the entire subject community. It seemed conceivable that these representatives could have been responsible for initiating change or making our materials more widely available.

Thus it was that in the autumn of 1999 we sent a postal questionnaire to 100 departments in the United Kingdom. We had just completed a successful conference and follow up publicity was circulated shortly after in an issue of the SSP2000 newsletter. Our intention was to maximise response rates by targeting our sample during a period when the issues were likely to be uppermost in their minds. The mailing also coincided with the start of the new academic year. This was double-edged. We reasoned from experience that teaching issues attain greatest prominence at this time of year and thereafter decline in precipitous fashion until the 'planning period' in the Spring when new courses are conceived and validated, or perhaps until external examiners have made their scheduled visits and commented upon provision. At the same time, from a practical perspective this is exactly the point in the academic cycle when colleagues are most preoccupied with teaching as opposed to completing questionnaires about teaching! A mixture of necessity and strategy drove the timing of the survey.

A second major stumbling block was the question of the sample itself, not least because it was far from obvious how to define the population. Given the fact that our funding and activities had officially been confined to England, what was the merit in broadening the survey to Scotland, Wales and Northern Ireland given the fact they had also been inspected under a different and prior regime of quality assurance? On the other hand, our project had in fact escaped the boundaries of geography. We had held an informal workshop in Wales. Teaching and learning issues had been discussed at two BSA conferences in Edinburgh and Glasgow. All four corners of the Kingdom were represented on the BSA's benchmarking panel. Since it had never been our aim to restrict our message to colleagues in England it now made sense to broaden our investigation of its effects. A more unexpected problem relating to the definition of the 'eligible population' was in identifying 'sociology departments' in institutions. We adopted a flexible line. Clearly sociologists are to be found in a variety of institutional configurations, many of which are largely cosmetic or historical artefacts. On the other hand there were numerous occasions where the project staff hit dead ends even in trying to identify a suitable named person for receipt of the questionnaire. Searches of websites failed to yield obvious targets. Phone calls to departments were met with redirection and uncertainty. In the end we relied on an imperfect BSA register of departments, a good deal of personal knowledge and some well informed guesswork.

We settled on a list of a hundred locations where we had good cause to believe that someone was practising sociology. Beyond this, however, we had another issue to resolve. Were we investigating the assessment practices of individuals or of departments? In other words was this a sample survey of sociology teachers or a census of teaching departments? In the event we decided on the latter, for a number of quite separate reasons. Firstly, departments were the unit of analysis in 1995–96 so it made some sense to stick with this. We had no systematic information about the practices of individuals from the TQA reports. Many departments had tacit or statutory policies about assessment that could override individuals' preferences. Moreover, we were increasingly convinced of the significance of 'assessment strategies'; a shorthand term for a concerted collegiate approach to the way students' performance was gauged throughout the degree. Some other studies in the higher education literature had drawn attention to the strength of departmental cultures in influencing patterns of teaching. In the event we received completed questionnaires from 57 departments. In the remainder of this chapter we offer some observations on the results.

The questionnaire was divided into sections. We needed to obtain the detailed information about assessment methods that the TQA reports had failed to provide. The second block of questions was devoted to this task. Before answering these our respondents were faced with a number of background enquiries designed to explore the ways in which assessment was organised, where responsibilities lay and what procedures were in place. We began by addressing one of the central themes of our project, namely the degree to which unitisation and modularisation have fragmented the practice of assessment. Asked to assess whether assessment was the preserve of individual module tutors or the outcome of strategic deliberations, 30 departments claimed to adopt a strategic approach. A further 11 indicated that there was some combination of the two, usually where individual tutors would design specific assessment tasks that in turn would be subject to more formal approval mechanisms. This might involve general discussion amongst colleagues or scrutiny by a teaching committee or validation body of some sort. The remaining 16 departments appeared to have devolved the decision fully to module leaders. A small number of respondents mentioned institutional constraints related either to credit transfer systems or the balance between particular modes of assessment.

The next two questions concerned quality control. Question 2 asked respondents to tell us whether assessment tasks (by which we mean here the actual content of essay questions, assignments or exam papers) were subject to peer review and to clarify further the form this would take. This prompted a range of responses that are summarised in table 3.1 below.

These responses put the answers to the previous question in perspective. While more than half of departments claim to take a strategic overview of the assessment process, the way it is operationalised varies a good deal. Less than a third of departments systematically review the entire assessment diet prior to students completing them. Around three-quarters of the respondents claimed to do some screening of some tasks, with formal exam papers taking priority. This probably reflects the historical significance of final examinations, but in more diverse modular systems it could be argued that they are no longer any more numerically important than coursework assignments and that such arrangements need to be harmonised. Beyond this it was notable that 13 departments only undertook peer evaluation after the event, through the committee structure. In these circumstances individual tutors retained a good deal of autonomy, although they were accountable for their choice of methods.

Table 3.1 Internal Peer Review of Assessment Tasks

All tasks reviewed by the department/field/group	16
Only exams are reviewed by department or group	13
Tasks receive informal peer feedback	9
Tasks discussed by module teams	6
Tasks reviewed by a Teaching and Learning Committee	5
Tasks reviewed by the Annual Review process	3
Use of 'double-marking'	3
Tasks reviewed only at Stage 1	1
No procedures	1
TOTAL	57

We followed this up by seeking information about the role of external examiners in this process. Traditionally the main contribution of externals has been in terms of the marking and moderation process, but as this has become increasingly onerous there is some anecdotal evidence that the role is mutating into that of the quality assurance adviser who looks at all aspects of academic provision. In reply to this query, 23 of the 57 respondents told us that all assessment tasks were seen by the external examiner prior to being printed. A further 27 reported that this was standard practice for formal examination papers. It is clear that academics still perceive a hierarchy of assessment modes in terms of both internal and external quality assurance. Of the other 7 respondents, 5 obtained external comments after the event, and the other 2 reported no procedures in this area.

Having established the prevailing patterns of administrative arrangements, we moved on to look for answers to our primary concern – was there any evidence of a change of thinking or major innovations in this area in the wake of the round of TQA visits? Question 4 invited respondents to nominate any number of ways in which the department had changed the way it assessed its students in the previous three years. The results are summarised in table 3.2.

Table 3.2 Changes in Assessment in the Previous Three Years

No change	15
Introduction of more coursework	5
A move to greater diversity	20
Attempts to reduce assessment overload	4
Harmonisation of word limits/greater equity	6
Introduction of more exams	5
Increase in use of learning outcomes	5
Greater discussion of assessment issues/provision of guidance to students	6
Introduction of Multiple Choice Questions	1
Cannot say	1
TOTAL	69

What these responses appeared to indicate was that the 'diversity' message was getting through in a substantial number of departments, though a quarter claimed that their practices were unchanged. The more specific examples offered by respondents were intriguingly mixed. Some (use of learning outcomes, the use of more diverse assessment tools) seemed pedagogically motivated; others (trends towards clearer communication and greater transparency of requirements) were more probably driven by concerns over quality assurance. Of course, the two are not mutually exclusive. In among the main message we found the counter-trend of movement back towards unseen examinations as a mode of delivery in a handful of places. We might speculate that this is connected in some way to growing concerns about plagiarism.

These issues were further illuminated by the data yielded by our next question. We asked our respondents to list the assessment issues that were of main concern to academics in the department. We were interested to get a different perspective from that of educational developers who are not always day-to-day practitioners in the classroom. The answers could be said to encapsulate the twin, and sometimes conflicting, themes of our project. Almost half reported concern with the amount of assessment and its effect on students, staff, or both (see table 3.3). Further evidence of the 'strategic overview' was apparent in the 13 departments where the overriding issue was the balance of the overall assessment diet. This frequently went along with some comment on making the assessment regime fit for purpose and being more explicit as a department about what that purpose was or should be. Here was a reflection of the orthodox educational agenda for improving learning through assessment by reducing unnecessary duplication and matching the tools more closely to the purpose.

Accompanying this, however, were many of the concerns about standards in assessment that reflect the quality assurance agenda of the regulators. There is little doubt that the phenomenon of plagiarism is perceived as much more problematic than a decade ago. Equally, the onset of modularity and semesterisation that began in earnest during the 1990s is now making its effects widely felt. Students and examiners in the non-state sector traditionally tended to be tolerant of the individual quirks of particular courses and of the different practices of academics. With the abolition of the binary divide and the extension of the credit transfer culture to most institutions, some of the side effects of this more transparent approach are becoming more keenly perceived. Whatever soothing forms of words accompany their introduction, the simple act of attaching numbers to courses with quite different objectives is bound to lead to some questioning of the consistency of such a currency. Demonstrating the equivalence between academic 'apples' and 'oranges' in this way is likely to remain problematic for some time yet.

Table 3.3 Main Concerns Expressed about Assessment

Overload on students and staff	26
Overall balance/clarity of purpose	13
Plagiarism	11
Standards/moderation issues	9
Comparability between modules	8
Fragmentation/progression issues	7
Poor student performance	6
No concerns/no response	3
TOTAL	83

This concluded the first half of the questionnaire. In the second section we were attempting to roughly map the make-up of a sociology degree in our sample of institutions. In part we were motivated by straightforward curiosity. It is often rather baldly stated that the HE sector has become very diverse and fragmented, making comparisons of any worth between courses extremely difficult. We soon realised that beyond our personal experience of half a dozen departments we had very little idea whether this held for sociology. The overview report commented on the triple strategy of essay, exam and dissertation, so we attempted to establish some rough picture of the overall pattern of assessment. This second section began by asking respondents what part a final year dissertation or project played in their degree schemes, recalling the almost totemic significance given to it in many of the TQA reports on individual departments. In forty cases this was indeed a compulsory element, while in an additional six departments it was either mandatory or recommended for single honours programmes only. A further ten offered optional dissertations and in only a single case was no provision made for this.

The next two questions concerned the weightings of different approaches within the curriculum. The first followed up on the dissertation theme by asking respondents to state what proportion of a candidate's *final year marks* was constituted by the dissertation mark. We phrased the question in this way to control for the effects of different systems of calculating degree classifications. The answers were expressed in different forms with differing degrees of explanatory annotations, but we reorganised them in percentage format and the results are displayed below.

Figure 3.1 Contribution of Dissertation to Final Year Marks among 57 Departments

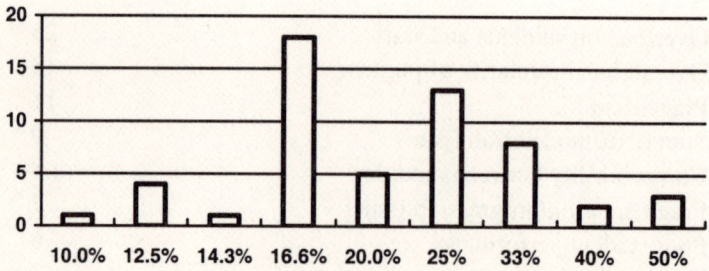

The most notable thing about this distribution is its spread. We have just seen that there is a general consensus that the dissertation is an indispensable part of a sociological undergraduate training. This said, the relative significance of that element for any given student will vary enormously, comprising anything from just 10 per cent to half a finalist's efforts. Of course, critics might argue, the results can be read another way. More than three quarters of departments set the dissertation at between one sixth and one third of final year work, that is to say between 20 and 40

CAT credits, so in fact the majority of cases lie within a smaller range. Equally these credit ratings may be artefacts of particular administrative systems rather than reflecting a conscious curricular valuation. There may be 'hidden weightings' in certain systems where a dissertation can be used to trigger a degree class decision. This would give it a significance that belied its small proportion of study credits. All these observations are perfectly valid; we still were surprised by the lack of consistency between institutions offering what on paper is the same qualification – an honours degree in sociology.

The next question asked respondents, in the light of debates over the 'drift to coursework' in the last thirty years, to estimate what proportions of students' degree work were assessed through 'coursework' and through 'examinations'. The boundaries between these two are not always completely firm but they are commonly set up as dichotomous approaches. What struck us most in the results was not simply the range of responses we received, but the trouble many of our sample had in providing the information. The assessment balance covered the full range from 95 per cent coursework and 5 per cent examination to 10 per cent coursework and 90 per cent examination. If our sample were representative of the sector, then it would indicate that the 'progressives' long ago won the battle over assessment methods. Twenty six of the 49 departments who filed a response to question 8 assessed the majority of student work through 'coursework'. A further 8 departments adopted a 50/50 ratio. In fourteen the balance lay in the other direction.

While these results were of interest in their own right, what surprised us was the number of these responses that were annotated with comments about the balance of assessment being decided by students' module choices or combination of subjects. Eight questionnaires were returned with the space left blank and comments such as 'it depends on student module choices', or 'difficult to say as some courses have a bit of each'. Another commented 'it is possible for a student to complete level 3 by all coursework: given the requirement that students must take an extended essay module, it is not possible to complete by exam'. Many of those who attempted estimates, accompanied these with the same sort of remarks.

These results demonstrate two developments that have taken place in the 1990s. Firstly, there is greater diversity in the assessment of modules and whole programmes, as standard 'templates' for courses taken over one academic year have been replaced by a multitude of new modules of differing shapes and sizes. Secondly, it is quite apparent that one outcome of this process has been that staff have simply lost control of the individual student's assessment experience. While educational developers have called for strategic overviews of assessment, the structural imperatives of the system have caused fragmentation, experimentation, and 'horses for courses' approaches driven by individual sets of learning outcomes. Neither of these agendas is without merit, but it must now be obvious that nor can they be simultaneously be accommodated with any comfort. Our project began with the aim of improving assessment strategies. What emerged during the survey was that strategic approaches to assessment might now be as common among students making their module choices, as they are among staff designing them.

We completed the survey by providing respondents with a list of less traditional variations on the basic modes of assessment and asking them to select methods they had used in their own departments. Aware that many colleagues make distinctions between assessment as a tool for learning and as a measure of final achievement, we allowed them to tick two lists – one of methods used in formative assessments which did not contribute to degree classification, and the other of techniques used for 'degree class' work. This yielded the following results.

Table 3.4 'Innovatory' Assessments used by Sociology Departments (n = 57)

	Counting towards degree	Non-contributory assessment
Open book examination	11	10
'Seen' examination	25	12
'Take-home' examination	6	8
Oral presentation	25	29
Group presentation	20	29
Report-writing	27	14
Projects	34	12
Book reviews	25	20

We need to be cautious in interpreting this table. Leaving aside the generic category of 'projects', no method on the list had been tried by more than half the 57 departments in the sample. It might be tempting to reiterate the assessors' judgement that half of departments still rely on the traditional modes of assessment. Of course presented in this simple way the data does not tell us whether it is the same departments that experiment with multiple methods while other departments eschew all innovation, or whether different departments each try a few different new techniques. What the actual data showed was that all but two departments in the sample had tried something from our list for the assessment of degree class work. Thirty three of the departments that responded to this question had used 4 or more of the 8 methods listed. A further 13 had tried making use of 2 or 3 of them.

Conclusions: Unanswered Questions

A number of lessons can be drawn from the experience of undertaking a survey of assesment practice in the sociology community. The first of these is just how surprisingly difficult it was to identify and contact appropriate people. Sociologists have tended to cluster into small study groups based on research interests. Aside from the newly established teaching and learning network created by the SSP2000 initiative there was little good quality information about the nature of undergraduate sociology in Britain. This low knowledge base was reflected in the basic nature of the questions we asked, and the provisional and limited nature of our results. Numerous intriguing questions were raised by the returns of the survey. Probably the major consideration is whether the departments that did return their questionnaire were representative of all British departments. It could be argued that the results are skewed towards 'innovators' and that places where academics were either indifferent or hostile to the notion of 'improving assessment strategies' were unlikely to respond. This certainly makes intuitive sense and if true would mean that the broader picture is still more traditional than our results indicated.

Beyond this basic uncertainty there are a number of empirical puzzles about the assessment practice of sociologists that would require further research. What are the factors that are associated with a department's take up of 'innovative assessment'? We might hypothesise that such departments will have a number of individuals either with a teaching background or a teaching qualification of some sort. We might additionally assume that, given the structure of academic careers in the past, many might be female. It would seem plausible that departments with stable staff establishments, i.e. low rates of labour turnover, might have more well established practices for peer review and would adopt a collective outlook. Alternatively such mechanisms might be associated with more bureaucratised structures where more formal meetings are a substitute for professional familiarity. A decade ago we would have expected that the 'mission' of the institution would be the major predictor variable. As staff have moved to and fro across the binary divide in the 1990s this is likely to have weakened its effect.

The unfortunate situation we find ourselves in is that we really do not have any firm answers to these and many other questions. It would take much more comprehensive survey evidence about teachers of sociology to allow us to make such claims. There is no obvious sign that British sociologists, either individually or collectively, are interested in gathering any. Sociologists of education have built an extensive literature on clasroom relationships and teacher-pupil interaction. Almost none of this is concerned with university education. Some colleagues genuinely believe that studying ourselves is too self-indulgent when there are so many more serious problems in society. Others are unwilling or unable to turn their analytical tools on their own behaviour and attitudes. Whatever the reasons, this state of affairs will have to change if the 'sociology profession' is to retain its ability to regulate from within.

4 Benchmarking the Sociology Discipline

JOAN CHANDLER

Introduction

Benchmarks are one of the new challenges to higher education. A brief look at the Oxford Dictionary gives some idea of how the idea of a benchmark has changed and become a feature of quality assurance. Its first use referred to the 'surveyor's mark cut in a wall, pillar, building etc., used as a reference point in measuring altitudes'. It was then generalised to mean a standard point of reference and more recently used to describe a method of computer testing. Benchmarks have now been adopted as one feature of the new system of quality assurance being developed by the QAA in its policy to ensure that the academic standards assumed by awards are made more explicit and more open to scrutiny. As such 'benchmarks' and 'benchmarking' have entered the discourse and increasingly the argot of academic communities.

Benchmarks and the Quality Assurance Agency

Benchmarks also carry bring with them new assumptions which are indicative of how the quality assurance process may change as a new system of academic review is developed and put into practice. Firstly the focus of review spotlights student performance on graduation, as judged against national standards and encapsulated in benchmarks. This marks a shift from process to outcome, a move from 'fitness for purpose' in setting the objectives of programmes towards a notional 'gold standard'. Secondly, Teaching Quality Assessment (TQA) came to be seen as flawed because of the apparent 'softness' of peer judgements and a lack of willingness amongst academics to expose failing subject areas within potentially failing higher education establishments. Benchmarks are thus also an attempt to at

41

least structure the judgements of peer reviewers. Thirdly some subject areas are more closely associated than others with vocational areas and professional bodies who have an interest in the curriculum and its relation to professional recruitment and occupational regulation. From a quality assurance viewpoint these groups and subject areas have the advantage of being more self-regulating and thus peer review is a more challenging process. Benchmarks can be seen as an attempt to generate a set of quasi-professional standards for non-vocational subjects, an encouragement for academic associations to assist in the production of national standards for all of higher education. Finally the practice of institutional visits, at the heart of TQA, was costly and the new system, of which benchmarks are to be a part, is claimed to be less of a burden on departments and institutions.

The Academic Origins of Benchmarks

Although they were not known as such, 'benchmarks' do have a number of academic antecedents. One strand of influence can be found in the development of a national framework within which graduate qualities could be mapped. Here there are two major examples. Firstly, a Higher Education Quality Council project attempted to identify the characteristics of 'graduateness' (HEQC, 1997) within a matrix of knowledge, skills and attributes. From this project a profile of graduate qualities was developed which 15 subject groups used to map their disciplines and identify the qualities of their graduates. Secondly, generic level descriptors have been developed and related to qualifications and awards (DfEE, 1998). Within this framework learning accredited at graduate level was described as reflecting the ability to:

> Critically review, consolidate and extend a systematic and coherent body of knowledge, utilising specialised skills across an area of study; critically *evaluate* new concepts and evidence from a range of sources; transfer and apply diagnostic and creative skills and exercise significant judgement in a range of situations; and accept accountability for determining and achieving personal and/or group outcomes.

A *qualifications framework*, another element in the new regime of quality assurance, draws upon level descriptors for the typification of output standards. The achievement described above is deemed to be that of the average successful HE level 3 student and as such should relate to the descriptions of typical or modal performance contained in the benchmark statements. However, most benchmark statements, including those of

Sociology, do not appear to be at this level. For example 'the ability to consolidate and *extend* (my emphasis) a systematic and coherent body of knowledge....' is seen as beyond the capability of the average honours graduate. As benchmarks, level descriptors and an award framework are being introduced simultaneously into quality assurance processes, the disjuncture between these forms is something which QAA will have to address and subject areas be aware of and reflect upon in their course design.

Another strand comes from debates within sociology. Albrow (1986, 1990), following a previous lead from Abrams, argued that the purpose of undergraduate sociology was not primarily to produce professional sociologists who would tackle the socio-technical problems of society but to provide a broad education which would intellectually stretch and better the person and prepare them to enter a range of professional occupations. In this sociology was to provide 'a core for a humane education'. Sociology is ideally placed to do this as it encompasses a range of perspectives from the micro social (as in the consideration of issues such as identity) to an international and comparative perspective (for instance on the forces of globalisation). Albrow noted that the intrinsic skills of sociology are so valued by other occupations that it forms part of the professional training of many occupational groups and urges sociologists to 'lift our skills out of the shadows and especially to concentrate on our comparative advantage in relation to other fields of study' (1990: 235).

However, Albrow also did not focus on the curriculum per se as he argues that substantive areas of interest shift and sociology shares its methodologies with other disciplines. Instead he focused on the qualities and competencies of the sociology graduate and identified these as the capacity for conceptual thinking, an awareness of values and the ability to apply sociological reasoning to practical issues. He then went further in providing a specimen grid of how a set of desired capacities might relate to the different elements of a curriculum. The capacities listed include critical and constructive capacities, scholarship, textual analysis, abstract logical ability, computing, communication skills, understanding other people, foreign languages, creative intellectual ability, report writing and interpreting visual material. One may not agree with Albrow's list but it was a start for benchmarking and remains a framework within which there can be continuing reflection.

Payne, Lyon and Anderson (1989) added to the debate with their argument that research methods was a core element within the sociology undergraduate curriculum, essential for those going on to be professional sociologists and researchers, and offering key skills for those entering professional employment. They noted the growth in the methods component of courses, the tendency of methods teaching to become more skills orientated, the incorporation of IT to facilitate analysis and numeracy and an expansion of qualitative methodologies. Burgess (1990) also identified the key role of methods teaching in the undergraduate curriculum but was keen to argue that a knowledge of method and familiarity with technique needed, for sociology graduate, to be embedded within a conceptual framework, geared towards the development of critical reasoning and linked to substantive issues and problems. For Burgess 'articulate sociologists' would be produced by a 'graduate training focus(ed) on the link between sociological problems, theories and methods'.

The Nature of Benchmarks

Benchmark statements define national expectations of graduate understanding and skills in relation to subject disciplines. These expectations are to be articulated within programmes of study within institutions, which in turn are taught and assessed within the various elements of the modules or units within a student's programme of study. They are designed to link together in a more systematic way than was commonly the practice in higher education the activities of curriculum design, teaching strategies and methods and the process of assessment. In this academic context benchmarks are broad statements which represent general expectations about standards, particularly at threshold level (the level of a bare pass) most commonly for the award of an honours degree. Benchmarks are framed in terms of learning outcomes and not in terms of curriculum intentions or the specifics of curriculum content. What is significant about benchmarks is the way in which they tie together a number of strands of academic activity and relate student experience and performance to the core characteristics of subject areas and to a broad consensus about the qualities of a graduate.

It can be argued that benchmarks do not mark a radical transformation of the way in which curriculum is designed, delivered and assessed. In fact embryonic benchmarks are found in the course documentation and in the self-assessments that were prepared for the round of Teaching Quality Assessments of Sociology in 1995–6. This was the starting point for my own FDTL-funded project on benchmarking at Plymouth. A sample of 15 HE institutions was contacted with a request for course/programme information. Eleven Departments supplied us with this information. There were some features common to these 11 programmes. All had three broad strands to the curriculum that can be characterised as theory, methodology/methods and the substantive applications; most offered the opportunity to undertake a dissertation or individual project and in the majority of cases a dissertation was compulsory. However within course documentation there was little attempt to explicate the links between curriculum, learning outcomes and assessment. The focus was on aims rather than outcomes. Again these were written more as aims than learning outcomes, were not explicitly tied to methods of assessment or embedded in a wider definition of the core elements of undergraduate sociology.

Another major difference lies in the inclusion of skills-based learning outcomes in the briefs for constructing benchmarks. The debate about the skills of sociologists catches the new mood of government policy as greater importance is attached to the employability of graduates. The emphasis is placed as much on what the sociology graduate can do as what they know. There are a number of further aspects of the skills agenda that connect previous and likely future debates. These include the relationship between generic and discipline specific skills, the level of research skills which programmes attempt to inculcate, the place of skills in curriculum development and the way in which the benchmark document may assist in the promotion of sociology to prospective students and employers. These issues are discussed later in this chapter.

Benchmarking Sociology

The development of benchmarks for all subject areas in higher education was part of a wish list contained in the Dearing Report and the subsequent ambitious programme of activity announced in 1998 by the newly formed Quality Assurance Agency. The 41 subject areas were identified for benchmarking, although this was soon to become 42 as Sociology and Anthropology were allowed to develop their own benchmarks. In the process three subjects, Law, History and Chemistry, were picked to pilot the process. They in turn produced three very different models of what benchmarks might be. Despite rumours of disquiet within the QAA about the real usefulness of benchmarks and continuing criticism from the academic community about their purpose, the plan to benchmark the remaining 39 areas was to be realised. As benchmarks were an element of the new process of Academic Review and this process was to start in Scotland in September 2000 followed a year later by the rest of the UK, the remaining 38 subjects were to be benchmarked without delay.

Thus new guidelines were issued and the remaining subject areas were divided into 2 tranches, with sociology included in the first tranch of 17 subjects, which were to produce an agreed set of benchmarks. The brief for the Panel was to provide a set of statements which focused on the following five aspects:

- The nature and the extent of Sociology associated with an Honours Degree.
- The essential knowledge and understanding of Sociology that should be covered in all study programmes leading to an Honours Degree in Sociology.
- The skills and attributes to be developed in students through the study of Sociology at Honours Degree level.
- Recommendations concerning teaching, learning and assessment of the knowledge, skills and abilities required in a Honours Degree in Sociology.
- The criteria for the threshold and typical levels of attainment.

The Panel for sociology was agreed in the autumn of 1999. It included representatives from all parts of the UK, pre and post 1992 Universities and a sociologist employed in a senior position outside higher education. It convened its first meeting in December 1999 and was required to provide a set of benchmark statements that would be published by the QAA in April 2000. Within sociology the British Sociological Association was identified as the professional body that would facilitate the work of the Panel. In this role it offered nominations, liased with the QAA representative, provided a conduit for communications and assisted in the process of consultation with members. The Heads and Professors of Sociology Council also provided another forum in the process of consultation.

This process ran in parallel with our own work on Benchmarking within the FDTL project on assessment practices in Sociology. FDTL, with its remit of dissemination, provided an important support to the benchmarking process. Under its auspices a wider process of information giving and debate was set in train. This work pre-dated that of the QAA benchmarking panel and continued up until the publication of the benchmarking statements. A one-day conference was held, events took place at the BSA Annual Conference and visits were made to departments by members of the benchmark panel. The subsequent use of the Heads of Sociology Council and the BSA website as a forum ensured that the process of benchmarking was particularly open in Sociology.

The process of consultation revealed a number of concerns within academic sociology about benchmarks. These are detailed below:

- There were fears that benchmarks were the thin of a wedge that would open up higher education to the imposition of a national curriculum. This was linked to the fears that benchmarks would fix what was taught in a mould that was too restrictive in breadth and too rigid over time.
- Alternatively there were fears that the benchmarks would be set at the rarefied level of generality, would be so bland, that they would not define the subject at all.
- There was a new vocabulary to be learnt. What did all the new terms mean? What were 'benchmarks'? What were sociological skills? What was meant by 'typical' performance?
- The brief for the benchmarking group emphasised that its benchmarks should relate to single honours undergraduate programmes. The brief therefore prompted questions about how subject benchmarks would be used in multi-disciplinary programmes. This was specially pertinent given that sociology is overwhelmingly offered within modular schemes.
- There were questions about how benchmarks would relate to the specifics of curriculum within programmes. Here there was a tendency to try to relate particular benchmarks to particular modules or units within a programme.
- There was also a general resistance to benchmarking as it was seen as another time-consuming and pointless monitoring task. It was seen as an activity which would distract academics from their real work, do little to improve the actual educational experience of undergraduates and perceived as yet another salvo in the on-going attack on academic freedom.

Approaching the Benchmarks for Sociology

Two of the concerns formed something of a paradox – if the benchmarks were too detailed they ran the danger of prescribing the national curriculum, if they were not detailed enough, they would be entirely without point. It was important that the way the benchmarks were framed steered a course between these two extremes and were seen as appropriate with the wider academic community.

The generic skills and qualities of 'graduateness' were an important consideration in the benchmarking exercise, but it was decided not to benchmark what were seen as generic transferable skills. There were a number of reasons for this decision. The definition of 'generic' varied greatly in published material. There would be little value in different subject areas identifying different sets of generic qualities. As benchmarks described outcomes all of which would have to be achieved by the successful single honours graduate, it would introduce a compulsory skills-heavy agenda to the curriculum. It was therefore decided to suggest a range of skills that might be encompassed by the curriculum but to only benchmark the specifically sociological.

The Panel debated the difference between 'threshold' and 'typical' performance. Were these candidates doing the same thing only more or less effectively or were they doing something qualitatively different? The benchmarks as they emerged assume that they are doing something that is qualitatively different. At the threshold graduates are effectively describing, identifying, recognising, selecting and summarising, while the typical graduate has gone one step further and is also examining, evaluating, analysing, assessing, discussing and formulating. The changing verb use in the move from threshold to typical is a guide to how the benchmarks may be operationalised in curriculum design and the associated assessment strategy.

The draft workings at each stage in the development of the benchmarks were made available for comment and scrutiny by all departments or units of sociology. During the process the preliminary ideas of the benchmark Panel attracted considerable critical comment. However, the majority of units and departments were largely content with the final draft. The efforts to promote ownership of the benchmarks amongst sociologists had at times been uncomfortable but had ultimately resulted in a fair measure of acceptance.

Defining Benchmarks

Benchmarks define standards in the areas of subject knowledge and understanding, cognitive skills and discipline specific skills. The benchmark document also includes discussion of the generic skills, which should be developed within graduate programmes, although these are not benchmarked. Examples of each category are taken from the benchmarks statements for Sociology and these are used to illustrate the issues departments and units of sociology will need to engage with as they evaluate and continue to develop their undergraduate programmes.

Subject knowledge

Benchmark	Threshold performance	Typical performance
An understanding of key concepts and theoretical approaches that have developed and are developing in sociology	Able to describe a range of key concepts and theoretical approaches within sociology	Able to describe and examine a range of key concepts and theoretical approaches within sociology and evaluate their application
An awareness of social diversity and inequality and their impact on the lives of individuals and groups	Able to recognise the patterns of social diversity and inequality	Able to provide an analytical account of the nature of social diversity and inequality and their effects
An understanding of the social nature of the relationship between individuals, groups and social institutions	Able to recognise the social relationships between individuals, groups and social institutions	Able to analyse the nature of social relationships between individuals, groups and social institutions
An understanding of the nature and appropriate use of research strategies and methods in gaining sociological knowledge	Able to identify diverse research strategies and methods and illustrate their use in gaining sociological knowledge	Able to examine a range of research strategies and methods and assess the appropriateness of their use

Cognitive skills

Benchmark	Threshold performance	Typical performance
Gathering, retrieving and synthesising information	Able to gather and summarise information	Able to draw on materials from a range of sources and demonstrate an ability to synthesise them
Reviewing and evaluating evidence	Able to cite evidence and make judgements about its merits	Able to draw on evidence to evaluate competing explanations
Developing a reasoned argument	Able to contrast points of view and discuss them	Able to evaluate the viability of competing explanations in explaining problems and draw appropriate conclusions

Discipline Specific Skills

Benchmark	Threshold performance	Typical performance
An ability to understand the nature of sociologically informed questions	Able to recognise sociologically informed questions	Able to formulate sociologically informed questions
Ability to use different methods of sociological enquiry	Able to practically apply basic research tools in a preliminary way	Able to practically select and use research tools
Ability to identify the ethical issues in social research	Able to recognise the ethical dimensions of social research	Able to analyse the ethical implications of social research in a variety of applied research settings

Ability to examine the relevance and application of academic and practical sociological work to issues of social, public and civic policy	Able to identify and select sociological work relevant to given social, public and civic policies	Able to identify and comment on the value of sociological work with regard to social, public and civic policy issues

Using Benchmarks

Benchmarks are intended to provide the overall framework within which the different educational processes of curriculum design, delivery and assessment are to be systematically related. They are designed to encourage transparency and coherence and the development of more explicit academic standards. The dual function of benchmarks has been highlighted in the benchmarking statement in that 'they enable the performance of individual students to be benchmarked in relation to specific learning outcomes; and provide a framework within which whole programmes can be reviewed'. Thus 'the statement of threshold and typical achievement may have different implications for the review process. The threshold statements describe the minimally acceptable standards that students must achieve to secure an honours degree. The descriptors of typical performance are less finely calibrated and describe the expected performance of the average student of Sociology at Honours degree level in the UK' (QAA, 2000).

The benchmark statements for Sociology have been agreed and published by the QAA. Units of Sociology will be required to engage with them as they prepare for the new system of academic review. Within this context, benchmarks have six broad implications for teaching and learning:

- The review of programmes.
- Dealing with multi-disciplinarity.
- The establishment of academic standards.
- The linkage of learning outcomes to assessment strategies.
- The promotion of the discipline in undergraduate education.
- Progression.

Reviewing Programmes

The benchmarks were designed as an aid to pedagogic dialogue within subject teams. In this light the pilot projects for benchmarks (Law,

Chemistry and History) have been trialed. The departments involved in the trials reported that they found the benchmarks helpful in the reflexive processes of programme review, especially the benchmark of typical achievement.

As well as their reflexive use, benchmarks should relate to the more detailed academic guidance that is to be articulated within programme specifications. These specifications are to describe the intended learning outcomes of programmes and their relationship to an indicative curriculum, the learning process and assessment strategies. The draft documentation on programme specification states that 'it is not expected that the outcomes defined by Subject Benchmarking Groups will totally supplant the institutionally determined outcomes in a Programme Specification. Rather it is intended that benchmarking information act as a general checkpoint against which the institution's own outcomes and processes can be referenced' (QAA, 1999: 9). One might expect to face the following questions when developing programme specifications for Sociology:

- What are the intended learning outcomes of the programme?
- How does the curriculum design and method of delivery enables these outcomes to be achieved?
- How are the learning outcomes assessed?
- How is progression in learning achieved within the programme?
- Are the benchmark domains and standards already realised within the particularities of the curriculum and how are they realised?
- What curriculum items are missing when they are compared with benchmark statements?
- What knowledge and skills does the curriculum provide that are in addition to the benchmarks?

One of the major fears about benchmarking is that it will lead to a national curriculum. This was not an objective of benchmarking and it needs re-emphasising that the benchmarks for sociology may be achieved in a number of ways and through a diversity of curricula. Thus it is not assumed that the benchmarks necessarily map onto specific modules or units within a programme of study. The benchmarks are deliberately cast at a high level of generality. This enables the diversity of the discipline to flourish and provides an opportunity for each department to express the particular flavour of its sociology in relation to its engagement with the benchmarks and construction of programme specifications. There are likely to be different routes to the same learning outcomes and a different mix of specialisms and strengths are found in different departments.

Furthermore, the dynamic nature of Sociology is evident in the way that it generates new concepts and tries to grapple with the emergent features of contemporary social life. It is also evident in the way in which the leading edge issues and findings of sociology are taken up, used and applied by other, often multi-disciplinary areas. The dynamic and unbounded nature of 'the social' is the lifeblood of Sociology and the development of new areas (e.g. body, emotions, new technologies and consumption) its continuing contribution to knowledge. The benchmark statements therefore should not restrict sociological perspective, freeze the development of the discipline or constrain its vitality.

One area of the curriculum that will require some particular attention in any review is the specification of a compulsory core and optional areas. If the achievement of a benchmark depends on students taking an option or an elective, this inevitably means that the required learning may be avoided and the associated learning outcome not achieved. A question that curriculum designers might like to ask is which benchmarked areas can students miss through their selection of options.

Multi-disciplinary Programmes

Another major issue that arises in the context of relating benchmarks to programme specifications is multi-disciplinarity and this is tackled next. Sociology appears in the curriculum in many forms, including single honours, combined and multi-disciplinary programmes and as an elective within programmes of study. The different types of programmes are likely to use benchmarks in different ways. One of the important issues is the extent to which the students opt for multi-disciplinarity and choose what is to be combined with what, as with many joint honours and minor programmes, and the extent multi-disciplinarity is designed into the programme by the course team. Where the student does the combining, it is suggested that each element of the combination should have a logic linked to the relevant benchmark statements. In the latter case it is incumbent on the course team to provide an *overarching* logic for the programme.

- *Single Honours and Major programmes* – it is assumed that all the benchmarks will be achieved within the programme. However optional elements may mean that universal coverage is hard to achieve. One solution is to be clear about the learning outcomes contained within the core/compulsory elements of a programme and structure optional elements to ensure the attainment of benchmark standards.

- *Joint Honours and Minor programmes* – where students follow a set diet of modules/units the relevant benchmark statements that are realised within the partial programme can be selected from the full guidelines. Optionality within part programmes is likely to be more difficult and here the advice is again for clarity over what are the core elements and the implications of choice for the achievement of outcomes.

- *Allied Disciplines* – some multi-disciplinary subjects such as cultural studies, and women's studies may see themselves as closely allied to sociology. Other multi-disciplinary subjects such as health and business studies which are seen as QA subject areas in their own right, but have traditionally drawn on elements of sociological knowledge. All these areas are free to draw on sociology benchmarks to reflect upon 'the social' as a dimension of their field of studies and to assist them in the construction of programme specifications.

- *Electives* – here benchmarks may assist in raising awareness as to what the particular learning outcome of an elective adds to a programme.

In addition, an advisory group dealing with the implications of benchmarking for multi-disciplinary programmes has reported. Their conclusions do little to help and they have generated a set of meta-criteria that appear to be yet another set of generic learning outcomes that in themselves do not assist subject areas to develop learning outcomes more closely tied to their programmes. There are two particular difficulties encountered in the context of multi-disciplinarity.

Firstly, the QAA have identified 42 subject areas for benchmarking but a question remains about what are the defining characteristics of a 'subject' in a system of higher education where course development has produced an ever-growing array of new multi-disciplinary programmes. An apparent paradox emerges when we compare actual trends in higher education. The growth of modularity, the creation of 'niche' courses and the preferences of students has led to a proliferation of 'new' degrees such as Sports Studies, Health Studies, etc. Such programmes are deliberately designed to draw on a number of distinct disciplines. The Benchmarking process reasserts the primacy of traditional subjects as the building blocks of academic provision. Benchmarks may not travel well beyond the areas in which they were designed – the undergraduate programme that is linked to professional qualification or the single honours degree in a clearly understood rather traditional discipline.

Secondly, programmes of study may share modules which draw on students from different subject areas. For instance a module in the Sociology of Health and Illness may be offered to those taking Sociology or Nursing degrees. Here the module may cover the same substantive areas but the learning outcomes for the two (or more) groups may be very different. The clearer specification of learning outcomes and their linkage to an assessment strategy may make some 'shared learning' more problematic. Greater specificity of this sort does seem to be at odds with the 'one size fits all' cost efficiencies of many modular systems.

The Establishment of Academic Standards

The articulation of 'threshold standards' is seen as one guarantor of academic standards. They make it less likely that students will graduate if they fall short of threshold achievement in the identified areas. There is a general concern that students may be awarded pass, ordinary or third class degrees when they have not developed the qualities of 'graduateness'. If this is what occasionally occurs, departments have to cease the practice. One reason for offering marginal passes rather than failure may be a sense of natural justice that after three years of study, for those who have stayed the course, candidates should have gained something to mark their achievements, however modest. This strengthens the case for the availability of intermediate qualifications, certificates and diplomas. It may also encourage the greater use of the ordinary rather than the honours degree.

In the sociology statements the verbs used in the descriptors are crucial. At the threshold students must be able to describe, recognise, identify, select, contrast viewpoints and apply basic research tools. In addition the typical student should be able to examine, provide an analytical account, evaluate, analyse, synthesise, assess and formulate. The learning process should enable them to do this and the assessment process guarantee that those who are awarded an honours degree, can actually demonstrate these qualities.

Another use of benchmarks in relation to standards is a developmental one. Once the standards within a programme are articulated they can be used to ratchet up either the performance or the expectations of students. Thus benchmarking may have a developmental role to play and can be used to improve practice and what students gain from their sociological education, without being unduly constraining either intellectually or politically.

The Promotion of the Discipline

Some sociologists saw benchmarking as an opportunity to promote the distinctive characteristics of the sociology graduate and proclaim them in a public forum. The subject had not always enjoyed a positive public image and here was an opportunity to highlight the skills and aptitudes of its graduates. Thus benchmarks have implications for promotional literature. They may also assist graduate students to articulate skills and knowledge more clearly, flesh out their CVs and promote themselves in the graduate market place. Hence there is an element of competition in the way in which subject groups benchmark their areas as they enable prospective students and potential employers to compare the learning outcomes of different disciplines.

A 'promotional' approach recognises that the great majority of sociology departments share common objectives with respect to the abilities and skills which Sociology students are expected to acquire. It draws on a history of reflection on the distinctive character of sociology. Three main examples come to mind. Albrow (1990) focused on the qualities and competencies of the sociology graduate which he identified as the capacity for conceptual thinking, an awareness of values and the ability to apply sociological reasoning to practical issues. Payne, Lyon and Anderson (1989) claimed that research methods was a core element of the Sociology undergraduate curriculum. Similarly Burgess argued that, for the sociology graduate, a knowledge of method and familiarity with technique needed to be embedded in a conceptual framework, geared towards the development of critical reasoning and linked to substantive issues and problems.

The Linkage of Learning Outcomes to Assessment Strategies

Here there are a number of issues.

- *Appropriateness of assessment* The assessment method must be appropriate for the learning outcome and as the learning outcomes vary so diversity is introduced into the overall package of assessment undertaken by the student. Benchmarks carry the connotation of measurement, but what are being measured here are qualities of mind and there are residual issues how benchmarks will be operationalised in decisions. For instance, all benchmark statements are likely to suggest that graduates will be skilled in oral and written communication. But the indicators of effective communication will remain to be teased out in the specifics of assessment criteria. As an exercise that assesses the range and appropriateness of assessment method one could select a benchmark statement, consider how these might be realised in the learning outcomes of particular course elements, the different ways in which they might be assessed and how assessment criteria that capture levels of achievement might be devised.

- *The use of positive assessment criteria* Assessment criteria are commonly devised in a top down manner and frequently expressed in negative terms. Their conceptual starting point is usually best performance and they describe how other candidates, while being more or less worthy, fall short of the best. Benchmarking aims to reverse the thinking about student performance, to start at the bottom, at the minimally acceptable achievement, and work up the ladder of attainment. Hence assessment criteria should capture what the students *can* do rather than what they *cannot* do. Threshold judgements are of course commonplace in the assessment process and all examiners have had debates about whether a particular piece of work is 'good enough'. However, current assessment criteria are rarely helpful in making this distinction and the decision to award a threshold pass carries little weight in terms of what they have achieved.

- *Failing a learning outcome* The brief for all benchmark statements is that all must be achieved within the course of undergraduate study. Although they may be part of the design there is no guarantee that students will pass all elements and achieve all the learning outcomes. One precaution would be to ensure that each learning outcome is tackled in more than one area of a programme. In addition it is important to note the impact of institutional practices in regard to compensating failure.

- *Modal or typical performance* Benchmark statements also describe the expected performance of the modal or typical student. Firstly, as with threshold attainment, the reference group for this performance is intended to be a national one, not amongst one cohort of students within any one institution. Therefore it is up to individual institutions to reflect on the performance of their students in terms of this national norm.

- *Policing class boundaries* However, in other ways the value of the description of typical performance to discussions of assessment is rather different from definitions of threshold attainment. The bulk of student grades cluster around the II.i/II.ii border and as the modal description broadly captures performance in this range it does not help to discriminate more finely between students in this region. Unlike the threshold statement, it does not describe a cut-off point. However, the distinction between the upper and lower second class degrees is often seen as the real 'threshold' that matters to students and to many employers. It is arguable that much more sensitive assessment criteria in this area would be more helpful as student performance is characteristically bunched around the II.i/I.ii mark, whereas only a minority of students perform on the pass/fail border. However it is not clear if the current system of degree classifications will remain and programmes are encouraged to calibrate assessment criteria in relation to the two reference points of threshold and typical.

• *A coherent assessment strategy* Benchmarking also relates to whole programmes and their specifications as these may be checked to establish how they fit within the subject framework. A principal concern is that programmes have a coherent assessment strategy that demonstrates how the different units of assessment cover the full range of learning outcomes. One consequence is likely to be the development of assessment profiles for whole programmes. Where the issue is how the benchmarks of different subject groups inform combined programmes, there will have to be decisions about which benchmarks apply and judgements about the coherence of these combinations. However, within all programmes of study there is shift of concern from parts to whole. This is likely to limit the choice that students can exercise in selecting elements of their programmes and the freedom of individual academics to choose the form of assessment for their part of a programme. Benchmarks may move control away from the student in so far as they imply a more structured framework which constrains choice within programmes of study. They also shift some control from individual members of staff towards programme teams in designing curriculum and assessment methods. On the one hand this could be seen as a further erosion of the 'individual autonomy' of academics; on the other it encourages a return to more collegial approaches to teaching.

• *Range of assessment strategies* The Quality Assurance Subject Overview Report for Sociology noted the wide range of teaching methods used and the narrow range of assessment strategies employed. It is important to note why this might be. It is certainly more than the issue of inertia and lack of innovation. Unseen examinations are resource efficient in terms of staff time and essays and coursework provide extant pieces of work that facilitate the process of internal moderation and external examination. In its identification of a range of skills and a core of knowledge Benchmarking is likely to encourage increased diversity of assessment strategies. However, some of the new and more innovative assessment methods may be more attuned to a wider range of learning outcomes. However, many novel forms of assessment suffer from a perceived lack of rigour and their apparent resistance to external scrutiny and verification.

• *Explicating the implicit* Benchmarking has been said primarily to involve explication of what was previously implicit in curriculum design and assessment but it will probably mean more. There is a nagging doubt that much of what has been valued in undergraduate study may defy measurement and fears that benchmarking may lead academics to believe that that which cannot be assessed should not be valued. Learning outcomes that refer to abilities or qualities of the mind may be more acceptable than attributes, attitudes and qualities of the person. The capacity to collect and analyse data is seen to be more open to assessment and apparent objectivity than the capacity to work in teams or sensitivity to ethical issues or empathy. Also the skills agenda may raise issues for students with special needs if their range of achievement is to be more broadly based.

Postscript

There remain some bigger questions about benchmarks. The QAA expects subject areas to 'engage' with benchmark statements whilst not simply pasting them into their programmes as a pre-set list of learning outcomes. However, it is not entirely clear what will count as 'effective' and 'ineffective' engagement.

The QAA has not only required the development of subject benchmarks, it has also produced documents which contain generic level descriptors and has developed a qualifications framework. All are statements of learning outcomes but there is no necessary link between them and it may be possible for a student to achieve the benchmarked learning outcomes for an honours degree in a subject area but not to have performed at the level of an honours degree. Furthermore individual institutions may have their own attainment agenda for what they see as 'their' graduates and these will have to be accommodated in any operationalisation of benchmarks.

A question mark also hangs over the shelf life of benchmarks. The statements themselves may have to be refreshed in the context of a dynamic discipline and any changing expectations of undergraduate education. On a broader level they are part of a new system, the third in ten years, of quality assurance. In this context they may have all the durability of yesterday's buzzword. However, perhaps it is not the benchmarks themselves which are important but the method by which government edges higher education towards a more utilitarian outcomes/outputs approach to higher education.

Despite the grumbles about the new methodology, it is unlikely that issues of compliance and resistance will be the real stumbling block for benchmarks. Rather it may be the fact that it is difficult to use simple statements to capture and measure the dynamic, complex and qualitative experience that is undergraduate education. Again if benchmarks have any value it may be as a foil for reflection rather than the aid to measurement that they were originally conceived to be.

5 The Limits of Managerialism and the Need for Collegialism in Assessment: the Case of Dissertations in Sociology

ANDREW PILKINGTON, CHRIS WINCH AND RUCHIRA LEISTEN

Managerialism and Collegialism in Higher Education

The transition in Britain from an elite to a mass system of higher education has been accompanied by growing government intervention in higher education and the adoption of private sector management systems and techniques across higher education institutions. While these twin developments – which to some extent characterise the public services as a whole (Farnham and Horton, 1996) – are not of course completely novel and while their impact is not uniform, there is little doubt that the higher education sector as a whole has experienced since the late 1970s significant changes in the way it is managed (Scott, 1995).

This shift can be conceptualised as a shift from 'collegialism' to 'managerialism'. Collegialism is characterised by high trust relations. Academics are in this scenario envisaged as scholars who can be trusted to govern themselves and between whom there is parity of professional status. Since the essence of higher education hinges upon the idea of critical reflection and the latter is considered to be intrinsically valuable, a 'communicative' version of quality predominates. Based on 'tacit conceptions of value and propriety in the academic community', quality is considered to be most appropriately assessed through a form of peer review which excludes outsiders (Barnett, 1992: 7). The external examiner system is the preferred mechanism of quality assurance. Managerialism by contrast is characterised by low trust relations. While academics are recognised as professionals who have specific expertise, professionalism itself is seen as a strategy designed to protect the interests of academic tribes. A more rational approach to managing is needed which emphasises the role of strategic management in setting objectives and which devolves managerial responsibility to academics for achieving specific targets. Since the value of higher education is deemed to be primarily instrumental, for example the production of suitably qualified manpower, an 'instrumental' version of quality predominates. Quality in this view is most appropriately assessed 'in terms of the criteria of economy, efficiency and effectiveness' and by means of 'performance indicators enabling comparisons and measures of achievement to be made' (Farnham and Horton, 1996: 261). The external examiner system by itself is insufficient for quality assurance and needs to be supplemented by other mechanisms such as subject review and continuation audit.

Collegialism and managerialism constitute ideal types. No university or college has ever been characterised by either collegialism or managerialism in their pure forms. Nonetheless collegialism and managerialism can be characterised as extreme poles of a continuum and institutions can be located at different points on the continuum. A broad, albeit somewhat crude, distinction can be made here between the pre-1992 universities and other higher education institutions. The former were nearer the collegialism pole in the late 1970s than the latter and their movement along the continuum towards managerialism has not been as extensive as the latter. Despite this important caveat, there is little doubt that there has across the sector been a diminution of collegialism and an intensification of managerialism.

The Higher Education Funding Council for England (HEFCE), along with its counterparts in Scotland and Wales, are 'the key agencies within the new structure of higher education'. Unlike their predecessors 'the new funding councils are agents of government, not buffer bodies' between the government and universities facilitating institutional autonomy. Their primary role in fact, as Scott demonstrates, is 'to implement the government's predetermined objectives through second-order policies' (Scott, 1995: 27) and – given funding cuts, increasingly earmarked funding and the extension of external regulation through bodies such as the HEFCE-funded Quality Assurance Agency (QAA) – the practical consequence has been some erosion of institutional autonomy and academic freedom. While we should not underestimate the extent of differentiation in a formally unified university system, the external constraints within which universities and other higher education institutions operate has inevitably resulted in a shift, albeit a variable one, across the sector away from collegialism and towards managerialism.

The most common response of academics to this shift can be characterised as one of reluctant accommodation. Outright resistance has been exceptional and indeed many academics, fearful that external scrutiny might take worse forms, have participated in processes of external scrutiny to ensure that they take the more benign form of peer review. At the same time outright endorsement has also been exceptional, with many academics irritated that their energies are being taken away from the core activities of research and teaching and instead spent on peripheral activities, such as preparing for subject review, which unnecessarily interrupt the conversational flow of the academic community. It is scarcely surprising that most academics have neither explicitly resisted nor endorsed managerialism. Dependence on state funding has inhibited radical resistance, while adherence to an ideology of professionalism has discouraged overall endorsement.

Although the central concern of this chapter seeks to demonstrate through a specific case study the limitations of managerialism and the necessity of collegialism in assuring quality, it should not be assumed that we uncritically endorse collegialism. Collegialism, as we have characterised it above, tends to assume that the academy should be a self-governing community of scholars and that the interests of the wider society in the advancement of knowledge and higher levels of understanding among students are best served by leaving academics to pursue their profession without interference. These assumptions are both naive and self delusory. In a mass system of higher education dependant in large part on state funding, academics inevitably will be asked to account for what they do not only to their peers but also to other often more powerful stakeholders (Evans, 1999). To pretend otherwise is to be naive. What is more, it cannot be said that the heyday of collegialism in practice entailed a more systematic approach to teaching, learning and assessment issues in higher education. Far from it. Left to themselves, academics have tended to prioritise their own research interests to such an extent that sometimes scant regard has been given to their role as educators of students. Indeed it has only been through the prodding of external agencies such as HEFC and the QAA that a more systematic approach to learning and teaching is developing. Professionalism has been attacked across the political spectrum as an ideology which serves to protect the interests of particular occupational groups, and not without reason. To exempt academics from this critique is to engage in self-delusion.

A Case Study: Dissertations in Sociology

The case study reported here results from a HEFCE Fund for the Development of Teaching and Learning (FDTL) project, *Assessment*

Strategies and Standards in Sociology. The results of the overall project have been reported elsewhere (Harrison and Mears, 2000). Here our concern is with one of the subprojects which attempted to develop a common understanding of the nature and purpose of the dissertation element of the Sociology degree and to construct valid, reliable and practical assessment criteria on the basis of that understanding.

The dissertation is an established form of assessment and it might be presumed that it follows a similar pattern to other forms of written coursework. However the dissertation is special in a number of ways that are well documented in the assessment literature. We might summarise these as follows:

- It is an extended piece of work, usually of at least 10,000 words.
- The question or problem is usually defined or formulated by the students themselves, albeit in close consultation with a supervisor.
- The nature of the task requires students to draw upon several skill domains within a discipline, e.g. to draw upon both theoretical and methodological knowledge, as well as the practical skills needed to execute the work.
- Though the dissertation is often integrative in this way, it still takes very different forms and fulfils different functions in different programmes.
- It is almost always available as an option, is frequently compulsory, and in some cases is seen as a symbol of 'honours-worthiness', either metaphorically or in the actual letter of assessment regulations.
- Dissertations are always second-marked, often by a member of staff with less area-specific expertise than the first marker.

Each of these features of dissertation work makes it more problematic and therefore deserving of special attention within any departmental assessment strategy.

Our particular project entailed academics from five Sociology departments grappling with a range of issues which impinge on the assessment of the dissertation element. Here we shall focus on our attempts to work towards a consensus concerning the purposes of the dissertation and to develop a more robust framework for ensuring the validity and reliability of assessment. These aims were addressed by means of two parallel strategies: through a series of inter-departmental workshops and through a small-scale research project conducted in the participating institutions. We programmed a series of activities into the workshops including input from external speakers and a series of marking exercises. In addition, preliminary findings from the research on staff and student perceptions of the dissertation process were fed back to the workshop participants and formed part of the process of reflection on both the issues related to the overall purpose of the dissertation and the validity and reliability of assessment.

The Aims of the Sociology Dissertation

A degree of consensus about the purpose of the sociology dissertation was evident from the start. One dissertation guide serves to illustrate what was generally felt to be the overall purpose of the dissertation:

> ...a dissertation...is an extended piece of sociological analysis...is the crystallisation of the methodological, theoretical and substantive debates...Finally, the dissertation is primarily a piece of independent research.

In the course of a lengthy debate, we spelt out these aims and drew out some implications which needed to be addressed in our assessment practices:

- First, the dissertation provides the opportunity for students to integrate different aspects of their previous study of sociology and thus consolidate their grasp of the discipline.

Students will have studied sociological theory, sociological methods and substantive sociological topics without necessarily having seen connections between them. The sociology dissertation obliges students to draw upon both sociological theory and sociological methods to explore a particular topic. With so many different things expected of the student, the problem in assessment terms is how to isolate each of these for the awarding of marks, or whether to adopt a more holistic approach altogether.

- Second, the dissertation provides the opportunity for students to build on knowledge previously gained in an independent, focused and practical way.

Students are expected to formulate their own research question, to gather and select material relevant to answering that question, to answer that question and to set out their results. In this way, the dissertation brings their previous studies together to contribute to the formation of a complex skill that could be called the ability to independently carry out and report on a sociological investigation. The fact that dissertation students pursue topics of their own choosing and proceed with them without recourse to shared lectures means that assessment is largely divergent i.e. 'the assessment tasks are designed to enable students to demonstrate individuality and diversity' (Brown et al, 1996: 19).

- Third, the dissertation provides students with the opportunity to produce an extended written report on the whole process of an investigation.

The students have, therefore, to display a capacity, not only to write in clear and accessible language, but also to demonstrate the ability to deploy an extended, coherent line of argument. While this ability is a generic one rather than one specific to sociology, students are expected to demonstrate it through writing and producing an argument that is directed towards a topic of sociological interest. This means that the premises and intermediate steps in the argument, together with its implicit assumptions, draw on sociological knowledge or knowledge gathered through methodologies recognised as characteristic of the discipline. Thus, although production of the dissertation is intended to show the world beyond undergraduate studies that the student has acquired abilities crucial to the gathering, management and reporting of information, it does so in such a way that illustrates that the skill is grounded in a mastery of a given body of knowledge and canon of investigation.

There are a whole host of additional problems here for assessors. Firstly, the ability to deploy an extended, coherent line of argument implies a marking criterion that spans different sections of the final product. This makes it difficult to simply grade dissertations by disaggregating, marking and reaggregating the separate sections. Secondly, the length of the product increases the likelihood that it will vary in quality, both within and between its constituent parts, heightening the difficulty of making accurate holistic judgements. Thirdly, given that the dissertation is a blend of generic and specific skills, staff have to distinguish between these and decide on the relative importance they attach to each.

While we found few difficulties working towards a consensus regarding the overall purpose of dissertations, the marking exercises revealed that tutors placed different weightings on the various aspects of the dissertation, with some, for example, prioritising the quality of data collection and analysis and others prioritising the sophistication of the theoretical framework. Despite the fact that we were able quite quickly to translate the shared overall purpose of the dissertation into agreed learning outcomes, we found in practice that markers still placed significance on different ones. What made matters even worse was that we couldn't reach agreement on the relative value of different forms of dissertation.

Because Sociology is a complex and diverse subject, it is not possible to prescribe one kind of sociological investigation as appropriate for all dissertations. It is clear that the cultures of different courses or departments may give a strong steer to the nature of final year dissertation work, insisting, for example, that this involves an empirical investigation. Alternatively, courses may allow for a diversity of approaches to dissertation work within a single unit, permitting, for example, both dissertations which are largely theoretically based and dissertations which are largely empirically based. While these two broad forms are of course overlapping, theoretically based dissertations typically investigate an aspect of the conceptual framework of the discipline, with a view to criticising, clarifying or using it and empirically based dissertations, on the other hand, have, as their primary focus, the deployment of recognised sociological methods of data collection towards the answering of a question generated within the body of sociological theory.

Why should the co-existence of these different forms of dissertation be an issue? Simply because self-directed dissertations are divergent enough already without introducing yet more internal variation into the process. The question of how to compare like with like is inevitably raised. The stock answer would be that programmes or institutions are evaluated in terms of their own learning outcomes for the module.

Where this becomes more problematic is in departments that permit different dissertation models within a single module. Two solutions present themselves: either there need to be separate learning outcomes and assessment criteria for recognisably different forms of dissertation, or outcomes and criteria need to be sufficiently generic to accommodate all approaches. In our project we took the second route and developed, as we shall see, assessment criteria applicable to both kinds of dissertation.

Ensuring Validity and Reliability in the Assessment of Dissertations

It is important to ensure that the assessment of dissertations is valid, that is, departments actually assess what they consider to be the learning outcomes of dissertations. In addition, it is important to ensure that the assessment of dissertations is reliable, that is, that it does not vary significantly according to the individual marker (Ashcroft and Palacio, 1996).

Typically, departments seek to assure validity by devising assessment criteria which correspond to stated learning outcomes. And commonly departments seek to assure reliability by double marking and moderation by an external examiner. There are, however, problems with assuring that assessment is valid and reliable through these means:

- The desired learning outcomes are not described in a way which allows the development of appropriate assessment criteria.

- Double marking is often not done blindly, with the first marker (who is often the supervisor) influencing the second marker.

- Assessment criteria are often weighted differently by different markers. That is to say, some markers are more influenced by, for example the criterion of coherence in argument than they are by the criterion of appropriate data gathering and analysis, while other markers take the opposite approach.

- The external examiner usually only sees a sample of dissertations and so cannot ensure consistency throughout the whole body of dissertations.

- Research which has involved marking exercises where internal and external examiners have marked dissertations blindly against specified assessment criteria strongly indicates that, in practice, there is considerable inconsistency in marking. This is evident both in the studies reported in Pepper and Webster (1998) and in Pilkington, Winch and Leisten (1999).

It is worth expanding a little on these problems. Let us first take the issue of learning outcomes, since defining these is the first step towards identifying what we need to assess. Although all the departments in our research project had documents dealing with the purposes of the dissertation, these were written in different ways, often saying more about what the module aimed to provide than what students should be able to achieve. Freeman and Lewis (1998) identify four methods of describing learning, each of varying use in assessment planning:

- Topic lists.
- Learning outcomes.
- Question lists.
- Performance criteria.

The first of these, topic lists, is the shortest and most familiar. It is really more akin to a statement of module content and as such is of little use to tutors for assessment purposes. The second, the use of learning outcomes, is now more common and is likely to become more so as quality assurance is more outcome-driven. These normally contain 'active verbs' telling us about the desired achievements of student, but they vary enormously in specificity, for instance they do not always state the standard to which a student should be able to perform a task or demonstrate an ability. When it comes to the marking process the third approach, a question list, might be considered more useful, as it allows one to provide more detail under each learning outcome. It also acts as a useful checklist for assessors. However, while this offers useful guidance it is still far from apparent how a marker should judge the relative importance of different questions. For this reason most assessors gravitate towards the fourth approach, the use of performance criteria. It can be argued that when these are written well they lead to more precise statements than any other method; they also merge content and assessment into one statement, ensuring complete congruence between them. Since these are so explicit, variations between markers should in theory be minimal (Freeman and Lewis, 1998: 64).

In all forms of project work it is essential that the guidelines clarify the extent to which it is products or processes which are the aims and which will be assessed. Some of the departments in our research project had marking criteria that either explicitly or implicitly mentioned the ability to make effective use of the supervisory process. It is not uncommon to hear colleagues invoke the effort made by students when negotiating with second markers. The following sums up many of these issues quite succinctly though we might not agree with the suggested solution.

> Disagreements between markers arise for many reasons, some of which it is impossible to do anything about. But there is one important difference between the first and second marker which frequently leads to dissent and which can be easily be remedied. The first marker is almost invariably the student's teacher or supervisor and will know the student and be aware of how she has tackled the project. The second marker is unlikely to know anything about this and will have to award marks without any contextual information. Some of this information is crucial to a fair assessment of the project. For example did the student receive a great deal of help in carrying out the work? Was the original idea for the work the student's own? Was a first draft submitted to and improved by the student's teacher or supervisor? While it is possible to mark a piece of work 'on its own merits' without regard for such information, assessment criteria usually include such factors as the

initiative taken by the student, the creativity of the student and so on. Such criteria can only be implemented with the knowledge of the context in which the work was undertaken. To give an example of the problems which can arise, a student could have left it until the last minute to start a project, then sought the advice of her supervisor for a suitable topic, been given help with references and experimental design, been given help with analysis and interpretation and been given detailed comments on a first draft of the report. The student might then submit quite a good final report. The first marker would know that little of this was the student's own work and give a moderate mark whilst a second marker would simply mark the report as seen and award a high mark (Gibbs, Habeshaw and Habeshaw, 1986).

The authors advocate the use of a 'Second Marker's Sheet' as an alternative to 'blind' marking. While one can see the intention behind such an instrument, during our research project we moved away from the assessment of process towards concentrating explicitly on the characteristics of the product.

The problems identified above point to a key issue: the lack of shared ownership and common understanding of the criteria. This raises the question of how departments can move towards a shared understanding of assessment criteria. There is, unfortunately, in our view, no substitute for extensive departmental discussion and development work to both devise criteria and to operationalise them. In our own project, which involved five departments, with seemingly good practices in assuring quality, we found considerable inconsistency in marking . We found that it was only through extensive discussion of assessment criteria and follow-up work which involved using the criteria to mark specific dissertations, first that the problem was identified and, second, that means were found to address it.

We began our discussions by looking at the dissertation guides in the five departments. These typically listed a set of lengthy criteria for different degree classifications from what counts as a first class dissertation to a fail dissertation. Thus, in one department, five general criteria (design, execution, analysis, presentation and general) were identified and up to eight sub-criteria were distinguished within each general criterion. These criteria are often unwieldy, being neither helpful to students in preparing them for the requirements of a dissertation nor helpful to markers in ensuring a consistent use of the criteria. What is more, in most departments, we found that the criteria had been devised in such a way that the first class honours criteria are taken as benchmarks and the others are derived from them. This has, as a consequence, the outcome that the criteria for a third class honours degree seem wholly inadequate for any kind of degree, since they concentrate on specifying what is lacking in the dissertation, rather than identifying honours degree-worthiness (see Chandler in this volume).

The process described below should not be taken as a rigid framework for the development of departmental policy and practice. However, it illustrates the point made earlier, that departments need to engage in a collective process of determining and operationalising their dissertation assessment criteria, if they are to be assured that their marking is valid and reliable.

Having identified early on the unwieldy nature of the assessment criteria found in the dissertation guides, we sought to identify six general criteria which we considered most central in assessing what we agreed to be the learning outcomes. Having conducted an early marking exercise which revealed alarming inter-marker inconsistency, we confidently expected to find widespread consistency in the marks awarded by markers. When we used these criteria, however, to mark specific dissertations, we found, to our disappointment, that consistency of marking did not improve at all. The new assessment criteria did not seem to be any better than the old ones for assessment purposes, whatever their value to students as a guide to what was expected of them. We responded by adopting various 'techniques of neutralisation' to explain away this inconsistency. Perhaps the inconsistency related to the inexperience of some of the markers? Perhaps it was a function of the fact that different departments were still using implicitly different criteria? Perhaps we were tired after a long day and were not concentrating? Eventually, however, we had to concede that inter-marker inconsistency could not be so easily explained away. Somewhat disturbingly we were forced to recognise that we still tended to weight the criteria differently.

Fortunately the story has a happier ending. After a lot of disagreement, we eventually reached a consensus across five departments. Further discussion resulted in the construction of two orders of criteria. The first was a holistic criterion that reflected the importance attached to the adequacy of the overall argument, its coherence, integration and use of data, logical progression and critical awareness. We concluded that a dissertation cannot be awarded a class of degree mark above that given to this category, whatever the performance on the other criteria. The second-order criteria were designed to pick up specific features of the dissertation (the research problem, use of theory, literature review, methodology and presentation/expression) which contributed to its overall coherence. These criteria, although second order, were nonetheless considered significant and it was concluded that a dissertation needed to receive a mark for three of the five second-order criteria that reflected the standard achieved on the first-order criterion, in order to achieve that mark.

We recognise that this sounds complicated. It worked for us because everybody signed up to the criteria and had been involved in developing them. Thus when we repeated our marking exercise using the new system we found that considerable progress had been made towards greater consistency. During the process of our project, it became apparent that colleagues were almost unconsciously making 'holistic' judgements about the overall product and whether or not it 'hung together' as a piece. In practice this was overriding the quality of individual sections. It seemed good sense to accept this and make the assumption explicit within the broader criteria.

Two Orders of Assessment Criteria

First Order Criterion

- 'The Argument' – the assessment of the adequacy of the overall format, its coherence, integration and use of data, the logical progression in the argument and critical awareness.

Second Order Criteria

- 'The Research Problem' – the assessment of the overall sense of initial purpose and clarity and prospective sociological content of the dissertation project.

- 'Use of Theory' – the assessment of the project's awareness of and grounding in, sociological theory (broadly defined or in the form of a distinct hypothesis).

- 'The Literature Review' – the assessment of how the project is located within a review of an appropriate quantity and quality of literature.

- 'The Methodology' – the assessment of the choice of methodology (broadly including everything from primary data collection to the analysis of secondary sources) covering its justification, ethics, application and the appreciation of its strengths and weaknesses.

- 'The Presentation and Expression' – the assessment of how well the dissertation is written and its conformity to academic conventions (referencing and treatment of tables and figures).

Once agreement had been reached on distinguishing two orders of criteria and how they were to be operationalised, we still faced the need to distinguish different degree classifications. We needed to do this in a way that avoided the problem identified earlier of their concentrating (apart from the first class) on what is lacking in the dissertation, rather than identifying honours degree-worthiness. In what follows, we indicate the outcome of our discussions of degree classification, using the two orders of criteria described above. We devised these from the threshold, which specified the minimum standards required for an honours degree, up to a first, thus avoiding the problem identified above.

First Order Criterion

'The Argument'

First Class   Extremely strong internal consistency making the project a convincing whole which addresses the original research question; evidence of originality and freshness of argument; impressive use of the information gathered to sustain the argument; critical awareness of the strength and limitations of the project.

Upper Second   Evidence of internal consistency which relates to the original question; use of the information gathered to sustain the argument; awareness of strengths and limitations of the project.

Lower Second   Evidence of internal consistency which relates to the original research question but with some weaknesses in the integration of different sections; use of the information gathered to sustain the argument but with some weaknesses in the integration of evidence; some awareness of the strengths and limitations of the project.

Third Class   Limited evidence of internal consistency which relates to the original research question with significant weaknesses in the integration of different sections; limited use of the information gathered to sustain the argument with significant weaknesses in the integration of evidence; limited discussion of the strengths and weaknesses of the project.

Fail   Lack of internal consistency; very limited use of the information gathered to sustain the argument, with serious weaknesses in the integration of evidence; no awareness of the limitations of the project.

Second Order Criteria

1 *'The Research Problem'*

First Class   Very clearly formulated research question with a clear sociological focus.
Upper Second   Clearly formulated research question with a sociological focus.
Lower Second Generally competently formulated research question with some sociological focus.
Third Class   Generally competently formulated research question but lacking sociological focus.
Fail Poorly formulated research question.

2 *'Use of Theory'*

First Class   Extensive and critical awareness of and grounding in sociological theory.
Upper Second   Clear and some critical awareness of and grounding in sociological theory.
Lower Second Generally clear awareness of and grounding in sociological theory.
Third Class   Some limited awareness of and grounding in sociological theory.
Fail Little awareness of and grounding in sociological theory.

3 *'The Literature Review'*

First Class   Extensive reading which has been critically evaluated and explicitly related to the research question.
Upper Second   Wide reading, with some critical evaluation and relation to the research question.
Lower Second   Appropriate reading presented in a descriptive way not explicitly related to the research question.
Third Class   Reliance on limited sources, with limited connection to the research question.
Fail   Overreliance on limited sources and not directly related to the research question.

4 'The Methodology'

First Class Very clear appreciation of relevant methodological issues; very clearly presented rationale for the methodological approach adopted; extremely systematic and appropriate information gathering and analysis; critical awareness of the strengths and limitations of the approach taken.

Upper Second An appreciation of relevant methodological issues; clearly presented rationale for the methodological approach adopted; very competent and appropriate information gathering and analysis; some awareness of the strengths and limitations of the approach taken.

Lower Second A familiarity with key methodological issues; a competent rationale presented for the methodological approach adopted; generally competent information gathering and analysis; a little awareness of the strengths and limitations of the approach taken.

Third Class Some awareness of methodological issues; a defensible rationale presented for the methodological approach adopted; some competent information gathering and analysis.

Fail Little awareness of methodological issues; an inappropriate rationale presented for the methodological adopted; poor and inappropriate information gathering and analysis.

5 'Presentation and Expression'

First Class Fully and appropriately referenced; well presented; very clear use of language.

Upper Second Generally, well referenced, well presented and clear use of language.

Lower Second Generally, well referenced, well presented and clear use of language, but with some errors.

Third Class Competently referenced, presented and clear use of language, but with significant errors.

Fail Poorly referenced, presented and unclear use of language, with serious errors.

Conclusion

We have argued that in the last two decades there has been a shift away from collegialism and a move towards managerialism. Despite the laments of academics, this has not altogether been a bad thing so far as teaching, learning and assessment issues are concerned. Our focus here has been on the issue of assessment and specifically the assessment of dissertations in

Sociology. There is little doubt that processes of external scrutiny have obliged us to give much more attention to teaching, learning and assessment issues generally than would otherwise have been the case. Both continuation audits and subject reviews have obliged institutions of higher education to develop a panoply of quality assurance systems and in their wake a plethora of documents spelling out the learning outcomes and assessment criteria of programmes and modules, including dissertations.

It is not surprising to discover therefore that the five departments which participated in our project all had dissertation guides and that these contained, at least purportedly, a list of learning outcomes and corresponding assessment criteria. Tacit rules had been replaced by codified procedures and all the departments had been obliged to give some thought to teaching, learning and assessment issues. And yet, despite the good scores all of them had received in their teaching quality assessments, what became apparent in the course of our project was alarming inter-marker inconsistency. Managerialism had put the issue of teaching, learning and assessment on the agenda but had not fundamentally changed departmental practices at least in respect of the assessment of dissertations. The documentation had improved; the policies had been formulated; the committees were now in place but something was missing. The 'administrative shell' of quality assurance was in place (Goodland, 1995) but less evident from our case study was the substance.

What enabled us to improve our assessment of the dissertation element was collegialism. Critical to the success of our project was the informal group discussion that drove the whole process forward. We had assembled a group of academics who had a clear and salient identity as sociologists, who believed in what they were doing, but wanted to improve it, particularly in the light of the reliability problems in marking that emerged at an early stage in the project. A developing sense of collective endeavour and emerging common understandings of what were the problems and the likely direction in which solutions lay provided the motivation to arrive at a conclusion which received common assent.

We believe that this experience has implications for the kind of quality assurance that is currently dominant in higher education in Britain. This relies heavily on documentation of, for example, assessment criteria without necessarily evaluating the quality or application of those criteria. Our study suggest that the assurance of the quality of assessment depends crucially upon common professional engagement on a structured but informal and collegial basis. Formal quality assurance, which involves much reading of reports and committee attendance, carries the cost of taking time that could be devoted to the more informal activities that we believe are crucial to the success of assessment arrangements. We would urge institutions and the QAA to consider the need to rebalance quality assurance arrangements between formal and informal processes in favour more of the latter and less of the former. We do not believe that this means that we should move towards a situation of laisser faire as regards quality assurance. Departmental discussion works best when there is a clear agenda. In addition, the cross-fertilisation of ideas and experience from other departments is critical to the success of departmental development programmes. We are arguing in short for a shifting of the balance towards collegialism which we think answers better to the requirements of stakeholder accountability than do many of the paper-driven formal processes that are part of the everyday experience of most academics in Britain. Weber pointed out how increasing instrumental rationality can lead to substantive irrationality. We are in danger of falling into that trap if we do not adopt a policy of resistance within accommodation and at least in part use our collegial identities to resist the dominance of managerialism.

6 Capturing Experience and Sorting it Out: Using Autobiographical Approaches as Learning Strategies in Social Science

BARBARA HARRISON AND NOD MILLER

Introduction

In *The Sociological Imagination*, C.Wright Mills suggested that the experience of the researcher was fundamental to the social scientific enterprise, and urged social researchers to place their biographical experience at the centre of their research and 'to capture what you experience and sort it out' (Mills, 1970: 216). A recent survey of teaching quality self-assessment documents (HEFCE, 1996) revealed that three-quarters of English sociology departments made reference to the development of students' sociological imaginations as central to their mission. There has been a major growth in interest in autobiographical and experiential approaches to research over the last ten years, and an increasing number of autobiographical accounts by sociologists themselves (for example Horobin and Davis, 1977; Riley, 1988; Mahoney and Zmroczek, 1997). However, we want to explore why, despite the growing concern with ideas of autobiography and experiential learning in a number of different contexts, these approaches seem not to be well developed as forms of pedagogic practice. We are interested in the extent to which models of experiential learning which incorporate the development of critical reflexivity on the self as a learner can be used in sociology and related social sciences. In this chapter we examine the potential of such approaches within the contemporary concerns of sociology, and highlight a

79

number of issues which arise in relation to these methods as learning strategies in higher education.

A brief statement about our own experience and our locations seems appropriate. We are both sociologists and we share an interest in the application of autobiographical approaches to research as well as to teaching and learning in the social sciences. The routes by which we have come to this mutual interest differ, as our current concerns related to different institutional locations and responsibilities. Barbara is in a Department of Sociology and Anthropology, and is involved with teaching sociology and social policy students. Her interest in these approaches has been stimulated by her interest in biographical methods in research, and by what she has learned about the value of utilising personal experience and critical reflection in teaching health professionals. Nod is located in an interdisciplinary Department of Innovation Studies, and has an institutional responsibility as an Assistant Vice-Chancellor for lifelong learning. Much of her research over the last twenty years has been conducted within the field of adult education, and she has a particular interest in processes of learning from experience and experiential learning (see Miller, 1993a; Boud and Miller, 1996). Thus in our collective work we have brought together approaches from social science and adult education. Our own biographies reflect our experience of investigating the use of autobiographical strategies in learning, where we found practitioners located in a variety of departments and related disciplines, and with different experiences of their own as teachers in particular. For both of us what has emerged as a key question is: how can we help students to 'capture their experience and sort it out' in the context of their learning in social science courses? We want to suggest that encouraging students to produce autobiographical accounts and to engage with theories and methodologies of autobiography (and hence to develop self-reflexive autobiographical practices) is one strategy towards this goal.

Arriving at an Overview

Our chapter draws on our own experience and data collected through the course of a project based at Bath Spa University College and funded by the Higher Education Funding Council for England's (HEFCE) Fund for the Development of Teaching and Learning (FDTL). This project focused on assessment and standards in sociology, but it was evident to us from the outset that it was difficult to separate out assessment from the wider context of teaching and learning. In this instance we will consider autobiographical approaches whether or not they are assessed, although elsewhere (Harrison,

Miller and Powell, 2000) we have given more detailed attention to assessment issues and practice. During the course of the project we were trying to ascertain the extent to which teaching, learning and assessment strategies in sociology and related degree courses in the UK employ autobiographical approaches. This has largely been achieved through networking with practitioners, with whom we have discussed pedagogic practices through a variety of means including personal conversations, interviews, formal group discussions, workshop and conference discussions, e-mail and other written communications. Our project has had the benefit of the preliminary findings of a similar investigation into life history within *History 2000* (Booth and Hyland, 2000). What an initial report reveals (Thompson, 1998) is that of 152 institutions which supplied questionnaire returns, 55 did not offer courses which used life history approaches, while 97 offered undergraduate and postgraduate courses which did. Included were a number of departments of sociology; 21 sociologists were represented in the teaching teams. This survey revealed a very wide range of approaches, including: the teaching of methods of life or oral history research; the analysis of existing autobiographical texts; the production of various kinds of personal history; and the use of experience to explore particular topics. Our own work revealed similar diversity.

The first thing to note about the kinds of material and practitioners we have encountered in our investigation is that the people involved are not all sociologists, nor are all the courses within mainstream sociology degrees, either at undergraduate or postgraduate level. It might be argued, however, that all the units/courses can be classified as having a concern with the 'social' and, as Thompson (1998) also found, many courses form part of multi-disciplinary degrees in which sociology or sociologically oriented material often plays a considerable part, including media, communications, cultural and women's studies, education and continuing professional development. We believe that this wider range of practices has provided valuable insights into the potential as well as the difficulties of the uses of these approaches. It is for this reason that we have used the term 'social science' in this chapter, in order to recognise the interdisciplinary context in which autobiographical approaches to learning are used. We believe there is sufficient commonality in teaching and learning strategies for such practice to be useful to sociologists. Thompson's study suggests that the use of autobiography and personal experience may be more widespread than our data indicates thus far, although it might also be the case that the study of lives has a more established role in history than in sociology. Our experience has been that we have had more people contact us because they would like to use these approaches rather than because they do so already. We hope the guidance in our contribution to a manual of practice for teachers (Harrison and Mears, 2000) will enable more to do so.

'Learning from Experience', Social Science and Postmodernity

Social science teaching is often conducted in a way that leaves implicit the theoretical model of learning being employed. Debates about the use of experience in social science teaching may be relatively recent, but the notion of learning from experience is certainly not a new one in the literature of adult education. The work of such frequently cited authors such as Dewey (1981), Freire (1972), Horton (1990) and Illich (1973) emphasises the importance of using experience in and for learning. A common assumption underlying much of the theory and practice of adult education is that adults learn throughout their lives, from their work and leisure, from their experience in social and domestic contexts, and from their personal relationships. It is recognised that educators need to take account of the life experience of adults in the design of curricula and in their approaches to teaching and learning.

Feminism has been an important influence on the growth of autobiographical approaches in research and in the learning context. Ribbens suggests that autobiography has been introduced into sociology teaching because of feminists' interests in 'exploring women's experiences in ways that may be hidden from view within more "traditional" academic formats, and/or as a way of exploring women's taken-for-granted understandings in order for individuals to be able to exercise more choice about their own lives' (1993: 83). She stresses that, for herself as a feminist, it is the way in which the approach allows an exploration of the links between 'private' and 'public' lives and knowledges and ways of knowing which is important. The issues of self and identity, which are relevant to women's lives, can also apply to other groups whose experiences have been similarly excluded. It is worth noting that in 1991 Ribbens, together with her students, published a pioneering monograph on the use of autobiography in teaching undergraduate sociology (Ribbens, 1991a).

Writers on postmodernism and education such as Usher and Edwards (1994) argue that the current interest in experiential learning is closely related to the increasing concern to come to terms with postmodernity. They suggest that the focus on experience as the basis for learning fits with such elements of postmodernity as uncertainty, rapid social and technological change, dissatisfaction with totalising explanations and grand narratives, a loss of faith in science and the rational, and the fragmentation of identity. They draw on themes developed in detail by Giddens, who suggests that in contemporary society (to which he applies the terms 'high' or 'late' modernity rather than postmodernity) 'the self becomes a reflexive project' (1991: 32). He sees the globalising tendencies of the present time as being accompanied by profound changes in social life and personal experience which result in efforts to construct and sustain the self through narratives of self-identity.

The current preoccupation with autobiographical exploration in the literature on adult education (see Miller, 1993b) indicates that adult educators are caught up in this process of self-reflection and self-construction. The shift in emphasis in current policy discourse from adult education to lifelong learning impacts on the contexts and identities of adult educators and gives rise to the need to rethink traditional curricula. These changes contribute to a growing concern with understanding processes of learning how to learn and with reflection on the self and on personal experience. Boundaries between learning and personal experience are becoming increasingly blurred as learning is recognised to take place in a wide variety of domestic, social and work-based settings.

Usher, Bryant and Johnson (1997) conduct a thorough dissection of the notion of experience as providing either foundation or stimulus for learning, arguing that any approach to using experience will generate its own representations of experience and will itself be influenced by the way experience is conceived or represented. Since any attempt to describe or reflect upon experience involves the use of language, there can be no such thing as unmediated or 'raw' experience. They advocate a conception of experience as a 'text', which can be read and interpreted, but which has no final or definitive meaning.

Analyses such as these are also to be found within contemporary sociology and provide a refreshing antidote to the rhetoric about self-actualisation and the search for authentic selves which until recently formed the dominant orthodoxy in much adult education literature. It seems important in our view to develop, as Usher, Bryant and Johnson (1997) have done, new conceptions of postmodern selves and to lay open to question the taken-for-granted assumptions about rationality and 'truth' which underpin many aspects of academic and educational life. At the same time, rising to the postmodern challenge results in some anxieties, for us at least, about straying too far down a relativist cul-de-sac and with uncertainties about an appropriate location from which to conduct an interrogation of experience. Postmodernist approaches provide no quick and easy answers to problems of educational practice.

Autobiographical Approaches and Learning from Experience

We now examine the ways in which autobiographical approaches have been incorporated into teaching and learning in sociology through the practices of teachers themselves. This requires an examination of what is meant by an autobiographical approach, and of whether or not learning from experience can be equated with the autobiographical. It is clearly possible to define autobiography in a narrow way as being only about the self in life, as encompassing a life history that is either complete or topically oriented; while personal experience and reflection can focus on very specific experiences of self and/or others, including the learning experience itself. Some practitioners, for example, argued that self-reflective journals or learning response diaries were not autobiographical, since autobiographical writing was itself a particular and identifiable genre. Stanley (1992) reminds us that the writing and reading about lives of others involves a constant interplay between self and others, and Morgan (1998: 655) has noted that 'in writing about ourselves we also construct ourselves as somebody different from the person who routinely and unproblematically inhabits and moves through social space and time'. It cannot be assumed there is a consensus on what autobiographical writing is. It would seem important, then, that in a teaching and learning context, assumptions which teachers have about their approach should be fully explained and discussed with students.

We encountered a number of different styles of autobiographical approach in the teaching and learning context, and there are also differences in the extent to which the theory and practice of forms of autobiography are taught as topics of study. One useful way to think about such differences that some courses (such as 'Life Histories' at the University of East London) are oriented toward autobiography as a genre, of understanding autobiographical narratives as particular kinds of texts. The Postgraduate Diploma in Adult Learning and Life Histories at the University of Sussex includes modules or elements of modules on autobiographical or life history research practice and on adult learning, but it also places considerable emphasis on an inductive approach where students use their own learning and educational life histories or 'academic stories' at the outset. A former student of this course pointed out that 'a course on auto/biography does not have to be auto/biographical'. Some practitioners teach and develop the approach and skills as part of a broader curriculum where autobiography may feature as part of both teaching and assessment. This may involve some attention to autobiography as a topic of study, and the development of skills in autobiographical writing. Students may be asked to use autobiography as a means of understanding themselves and the topic of inquiry; they may also be asked to examine autobiography as it has been used by others. For example, a core MA module at Bradford and Ilkley College, *Understanding Personal and Organisational Change in Community Settings*, explicitly orients to autobiography and biography in teaching and assessment in order to demonstrate the intersection with social structure and to facilitate both the academic learning of sociology and personal development.

Here we begin to see a different model of the use of autobiographical approaches where there is an explicit sociological rationale for it as a way of demonstrating and understanding the intersection between the individual (self) and the social structure. In this sense autobiographical approaches are tools that aid the acquisition of knowledge and learning about areas of substantive and theoretical concern to the module or course. Here might also be included Ribbens's practice on a course in gender inequality, where students present aspects of personal experience in small group contexts within seminars, and 'are *invited* to use autobiography as the basis of their assessed sociological essays' (1993: 82, author's emphasis). In a course at the University of Glamorgan in *Developments in Social Theory* (Oerton, 1999), students are required: to keep a self-reflexive journal, or 'an autobiographical account of daily life', for the duration of the course; to produce one piece of course work that consists of a critical analysis of that journal writing; and to write an analysis of the production of self (and others') identities through theoretical work encountered on the module (focusing on, for example, consumption practices, changing moralities or globalisation).

At the other end of the spectrum are those modules or courses in which students are encouraged or permitted to draw on personal experience or lives as part of an approach to learning. Nicole Matthews at Liverpool John Moores University uses this approach to facilitate 'deep learning'[1] in her module *Debating Gender and the Media*. Here students are encouraged to write short assessed response papers to the seminar and related reading and to refer to debates surrounding the topic, to other modules and to their own experience. A personal response to the reading is also encouraged. In addition there are a number of courses, often professionally-based or – related, such as those in counselling, community development, education, nursing and social work, where reflective skills and their development, which by necessity also involve the students' own experiences in placements, group work and so on, are key elements. Typically these involve students keeping learning diaries or journals, or constructing different forms of portfolio. These bear some similarity to the research diaries or reflective field notes which students are encouraged to use in some sociological research methods courses.[2] The focus may be more on developing skills of critical reflection and evaluation, and there is also often a strong emphasis on personal development, with the autobiographical element viewed as a tool enabling such personal growth as a key element in learning.

There are thus different motivations among practitioners for the adoption of these varied approaches as part of their teaching and learning strategies. Nicole Matthews (1998), for example, stresses the value of such approaches in giving students some control over the learning process. The response paper approach to assessment was designed to achieve this objective as well as to connect the theories students were learning to their own personal experience. Other practitioners, such as a team at Bradford and Ilkley College, argue that their use of the autobiographical approach is 'sociologically driven as opposed to learning theory driven'. However, this team draws on a model of learning which is 'very much about connecting with experience and moving things from there in order to engage with theory and relate theory to practice'. It is evident from a number of different discussions we have had with practitioners that the boundaries between the autobiographical component and the discipline-based content poses considerable difficulties. For teachers wanting to allow student choice and control, there is still a curriculum to be followed, academic skills to be developed, and sociological or other theoretical ideas to be engaged with and presented for assessment. As one practitioner described it 'we don't want to talk in terms of these rigid boundaries, but we do want some sociology and people are pulling it into individual psychologising very frequently'. We return to this theme as one of the issues in the use of autobiographical approaches in learning in later sections.

It is evident that autobiographical approaches are used throughout the different levels of undergraduate programmes, and that they also feature in postgraduate courses. In a number of contexts, the first year of academic study was viewed as particularly appropriate for using this approach to learning. Teachers considered it offered a way of developing skills of learning; and here it was used mainly in seminars and workshops and rarely assessed. In using forms of autobiography in teaching and learning a number of practitioners emphasise the importance of 'sharing of experiences' as a key element in the strategy. This requires some deconstruction since it is clear that 'experience' encompasses a similar range of interpretations as the different approaches to autobiography do. On the one hand it can refer to the experience of working in groups, typically in workshops or seminars, and the group is the experience that is shared, and analysing these group experiences is what the learning is oriented to. An alternative approach is where individual experiences of either the same or different events in the present or in past lives are written and presented.

It is this which is shared and drawn upon in the learning context. These alternative approaches also bring their own difficulties. Group experiences may develop understanding of group processes and dynamics, and a critical reflection of these can lead to self-evaluation, but they may be limited in their ability to realise an awareness of theoretical or conceptual lines of thinking outside of this limited context. An emphasis on the importance of experience can lead students to reify the concept as meaning that they must have experienced something personally. For example, one practitioner reported that a group of all-white students argued they were unable to talk about the exclusion of black women from the media from personal experience, yet it can also be argued they still have experiences of the representation of black women in the media. Equally, as another group pointed out in discussion, such a stress on experience can result in one student, such as one with a physical disability, carrying the burden of speaking about that experience, and so while one person's experience can be a shared experience in one sense it might not then become a common learning experience. This points to a limitation in the use of autobiography in teaching and learning. The approach may make it difficult to explore social structures which are outside the experience of the learners concerned, and/or it can leave learners with particular experiences exposed to detailed scrutiny by other students in the group. It can result in some students (often younger ones) feeling they have had not had enough experiences of life and have nothing to say, compared, as one teacher summarised it, to those 'rattling on about their personal lives, hysterectomies and divorces'. These issues suggest it is important to discuss both how people can and should appreciate the experiences of others, and to establish an equality of value in what students choose to use as their experiences. One anecdote of relevance here was recounted by a practitioner: 'One student said to his friends that he had to write the story of his life. His friends replied that first he had to "get a life".'

The development of autobiographical approaches in higher education may be a response to an increasing diversity in the student population. Teachers note that students increasingly bring a wealth of experiences with them, but recognise that confidence and skills in academic analysis may be new and, to some, daunting. Again, the *History 2000* project suggested that many teachers considered autobiographical approaches particularly suited to mature students (who also seemed to find it 'easier' than younger students) and to be favoured more by women. In Women's Studies courses such approaches have been accepted for much longer, and in other social science courses the use of autobiographical approaches tends to be concentrated in some areas rather than others. It is perhaps unsurprising that many of the courses which use these methods are concerned with gender, because there is an established role for personal narratives within feminist theory and practice and women's studies; women's own lives are seen to articulate both 'private' and 'public' domains of gender oppression. However, its usefulness pedagogically has also been emphasised by male teachers. One, for example, talked about using it to try to encourage young men to talk about particular topics, in this case their experience of sport 'which they take utterly for granted. They do a module on sport because they are interested in sport and that's exactly the reason why I don't want them to do it. So it can be a way of getting them to think about sport as a sociological topic'. Similarly another practitioner felt that 'it isn't just about women and men, it doesn't neatly fall into women being more personal and men being less'. Teachers report that the acceptance of and enthusiasm for these approaches varies considerably among learners. So too does the ability to reflect on, write about, and analyse personal experience. However, those who experience difficulties or who do not respond positively are in the minority. Learners' views can also change over time. Some learners report that they find reflection on experience 'hard work but worth it in the end'. One group of staff noted a range of responses from the students who 'loved doing it' because of the opportunity to write about themselves, to those who say they 'hated doing it' but were in retrospect very glad that they did.

Issues and Dilemmas in the Practice of Autobiography as a Form of Learning

We now move to an examination of a number of key issues and address them through the data we have collected to date. The issues are:

* the extent to which autobiography is seen as 'proper' sociology or social science;
* concerns about personal exposure in autobiography, and related questions of confidentiality and privacy;
* dilemmas of assessment;
* issues of authenticity.

Autobiography as 'Proper' Sociology

Despite a relative scarcity of teachers who use the approach in mainstream sociology courses, some of the practitioners we have talked to indicate that there has been a change in the acceptability of autobiographical approaches. A colleague associated with one long-established course that uses this approach within an MA module noted that in the early 1990s, when it was first validated, 'the approach was queried and challenged and actually nearly put the course in danger'; the staff had found themselves having to engage in writing additional papers and developing their own defence, because '… it certainly wasn't seen as a common or necessarily valid approach at that stage'. The *History 2000* project data also indicates that the development of life history approaches has occurred mainly since the early 1990s.

It might well be that the absence of widespread use of autobiographical approaches is in part due to a tendency for such an approach to be seen as 'not proper sociology' or as acceptable formats for learning and teaching, since some authors (Gibbs, 1992; Brown and Glasner, 1999) have noted that there is still a reliance on a single and often traditional approach to both teaching methods and modes of assessment. One of our informants suggested that it was not just pedagogic practice in this sense that was important, but the way in which much of the core curriculum of sociology is approached. He argued it does not incorporate making sense of everyday situations, and thus personal experiences of everyday life are not envisaged as a forum to which the more formal conceptual tools can be applied. Another of our informants also expressed concern about the presentation of social phenomena as amenable to being placed in neat and tidy categories; she said, 'Life is just messy. I know we might all want to be totally rational and totally cut off from all this messiness, but what sort of sociology is that?'.

For those teachers who use autobiographical methods it is clear that the learning of ideas and the understanding of theory are the primary aims. Thus they share with autobiographical researchers philosophical assumptions about the 'socialness' of subjectivity and the social connections and structures that are embedded in and can be discerned from individual lives. Thus there is no strong distinction between the individual and the social, and the justification for autobiography as a mode of understanding and writing sociology is clear. Ribbens articulates her approach in the following way:

> By insisting on a focus on core themes of the course I am requiring that they enter a dialogue with established sociological issues, concepts and literature. How this dialogue occurs – between the open-ended 'personal' and the established 'sociological' – varies greatly from one essay to another, and I am sometimes faced with difficult decisions about what I will accept and defend as 'sociological' writing (1993: 82).

On a number of occasions the role of autobiography within the broader context of academic discourse provided for debate about the expectations with respect to both the discipline and in relation to academic skills which students were expected to demonstrate. A piece of autobiographical work then should be assessed on the same criteria, it could be argued, as any other piece of sociological work: 'coherence, its demonstration of understanding of concepts, how analytical they are and so on'. As one women's studies practitioner recounted 'we get whole loads of wonderful description but they had not applied any theory to it at all and that on its own is worthless...It's not worthless as a piece of writing but as a piece of sociological writing it's worthless'. Another workshop participant argued 'the student should be able to identify and demonstrate their understanding of theoretical concepts and then be able to use autobiographical experience to unpack those theoretical concepts...show these theoretical principles at work in practice'. Whether or not autobiographical methods are regarded as 'good' sociology is also related to viewing them as part of a longer-term process, even within the constraints of semester-length courses. Ribbens (1991: 33) for example argues that 'autobiographical essays are less likely to be adequate as sociology if the writer does not allow her/himself the space to work on written material over a period of time, as a way of developing greater reflexivity about its emotional content'.

However, the acceptance of subjectivity and the growth of autobiographical approaches within sociology and allied disciplines can still meet with opposition on the grounds that it is not 'proper' sociology, or that it is not 'academic' work. One of our respondents reported how some of her colleagues had expressed fears about the possible consequences of encouraging students to bring their personal experiences into their sociological studies:

> there were some people who thought that I was going to be unleashing or opening the floodgates onto totally unacademic irrelevant stuff. They said that once people start talking about their own experiences they will never stop, and they wouldn't make academic connections. But that's not what happened at all.

Some practitioners suggested that it was concerns about possible reactions from external examiners which were used to argue against the introduction of autobiographical approaches into the social science curriculum. However, we also had reports of external examiners who were supportive of these innovations when they encountered them. Teachers also noted that in student feedback many learners acknowledged the benefits to them in terms of 'stimulating reading of essential literature', and 'proving our understanding'.

Dangers of Personal Exposure and Ethical Concerns of Confidentiality and Privacy

It is important to acknowledge that autobiographical approaches are perceived as carrying dilemmas and dangers for staff and students. Reflecting, revealing and writing about one's life can be difficult to do; it can also be personally challenging, emotionally fraught and painful. For many teachers, having access to aspects of their students' lives is also problematic. In the process teachers may have used their own lives, either as part of teaching what is involved in 'doing autobiography' or as part of their commitment to dialogue within the learning process. One colleague we interviewed had stopped presenting her life to students and analysing it sociologically as a case study because she felt 'very uncomfortable with it now' although at the beginning this practice had not presented her with problems. She thought the danger was that such presentations were 'almost like putting my life history in tablets of stone' rather than offering an interpretation at one point in time. It is clear that many practitioners think seriously and responsibly about this issue. In some cases there has been a realisation that there are potential problems with the emotionality that can accompany forms of revelatory personal material. These issues are complex, and there are a variety of responses to questions about how to deal with emotions. Some course teams will treat emotions as necessary parts of the learning process, and there will be acceptable outlets for dealing with them. Others, however, are inhibited, either because they feel ill-qualified to deal with the consequences or because they are concerned about the additional demands such personal and often individual forms of support dealing with such emotions may require. This is despite a recognition that there may be therapeutic effects which follow from students articulating and analysing negative experiences (Thompson, 1998: 12–13).

The kinds of dilemmas which arise in relation to personal revelation can be dealt with more easily where there is a team of staff sharing teaching responsibilities on a module or course, or where there is a culture which supports this kind of work. One of our informants spoke in terms of 'a strong impulse in this college to look at yourself and be what we call a reflective practitioner ... and what we are assessing is the students' ability to look at their own work'. It could be a lonely path for individuals who step out on their own using autobiographical approaches, but there is little doubt even here that enthusiasm and positive feedback from students act as vindication. We have surmised that these various dimensions of safety and the absence of a local ethos may be inhibiting factors that account in part for the considerable numbers of teachers who wish to use the approach, but have not done so as yet.

A number of issues related to safety arise in relation to autobiographical material in teaching and learning. Some of them are similar to those which the researcher has to consider (see Harrison and Lyon, 1993). It seems that practitioners have adopted a number of different approaches to dealing with the extent to which autobiographical material will become public knowledge. In many teaching situations forms of presentation, peer review and group discussion are used. Some colleagues consider these practices to be unproblematic while others take great care that the kind of material that is released into the discussion is controlled by the students themselves. So, for example, students may be asked to do a piece of autobiographical writing in private, but then be given a choice about what they reveal in the discussion which follows. In some courses, especially those running for more than one semester, a developmental approach can be used to build up skills and confidence whilst also observing some ground rules. At Bradford and Ilkley the students' autobiographical portfolios are regarded as highly confidential, so peer sharing is encouraged but not compulsory. A degree of trust has to develop between students and staff, especially in courses that require the submission of personal portfolios, learning diaries or reflective journals. Even if these are not marked (and they sometimes are) they will be seen by staff, and discussed in tutorials and feedback sessions. Respect for others, students and teachers alike, is also an important element of trust. As one tutor put it at the outset of her module on *Issues in Mental Health and Illness*, 'It is particularly important that everyone on this module be treated with great respect. I want us all to be able to be as open or as private as feels appropriate about our own, our families' and loved ones' experiences'.

We have interviewed colleagues who have emphasised that autobiographical accounts implicate other people, so that there also are issues of confidentiality of which students must take account. Where placements or work issues feature in students' work this is of particular importance, and dilemmas have arisen in some isolated instances where placement supervisors have asked for access to the learning diary. If placements have been problematic it will be appropriate for students to reflect on the difficulties encountered in their diaries. This generally seems to be dealt with either by negotiating expectations about access before the placement, or by producing two alternative diaries. What seems to be at the core of ideas of what is ethical practice in such learning situations is that students are in control of what and how much they reveal to others, although for some practitioners this does not mean they can choose to opt out of the exercise altogether.

Dilemmas of Assessment

One of the most difficult aspects of the autobiographical approach to teaching and learning seems to be the extent to which it should feature in assessment. Particularly in those courses associated with the early stages of a degree programme, the method functions only within the teaching situation and is not assessed. In nearly all the examples we have examined, there are no requirements for students to submit for assessment all of their autobiographical work, whether this work takes the form of learning diaries, portfolios, response papers, elements of life histories or autobiographical writing. Considerable emphasis seems to be put on two principles as a guide to the role of autobiography in assessment: first, that students should be able to make links between theory and practice, and second, that students are able to recognise in their personal lives, with their transitions and trajectories, key concepts of the discipline being studied.

In nearly all of the assessment types we have examined so far the autobiographical element is a supporting resource for the piece of work which carries the weight of the assessment. It is easy to understand why this is the case. As one practitioner put it: 'you don't want to be marking somebody's life; you know, your life gets 60 and your life gets 72 ... the more spectacular the life the more spectacular the mark'. But while teachers generally agree about the importance of the application of these autobiographical elements to sociological understanding, or to the theory-practice relationship, they also acknowledge that they sometimes find assessment difficult when they know the work and effort that has gone into the production of the autobiographical element. One teacher related a long discussion by staff concerning an essay in which 'someone who had a deep awareness of themselves and had written a deeply personal essay' had been failed because 's/he could not relate it to theory at all'. Where autobiographical approaches are used in assessment, as with the *History 2000* respondents, they are viewed as central to the learning process. This, however, is also part of a wider commitment to participatory and student-centred models of teaching and learning.

Issues of Authenticity

In many of the contexts in which we discussed autobiography as a learning strategy, participants would return to what we have called issues of authenticity. Essentially these discussions centred on whether or not fabrication, or the writing of a 'fictional' account of a life, was a concern, and how relevant was it for the student to 'tell the truth'. That such a debate exists suggests there is a distinction to be made between autobiography and autobiographical styles of writing.

There are other dimensions of the debate too. In one case, a participant argued that he 'was not too worried about the fiction element really because if they can write such a powerful piece of fiction that you can empathise with it that's okay'. Another felt that if the main purpose was engagement with theoretical frameworks 'fictional' biographical events could give some kind of value-added to the former. If however, its purpose was to comprehend what *really* touched someone and to view that person as, part of history, then authenticity in the form of 'truth' was important. More problematic might be the student whose experience of 'deviance' for example, consisted of living in a house full of smokers, compared to the student who has a history of abuse of recreational drugs and who has been busted. There may be a tendency to think that the mundane cannot be the subject of an interesting life, and this relates to the issues raised above about the idea of 'experience'. As one learner described it 'the notion of experience must be deconstructed and seen as imbued with multiple realities'. Some argue that we as teachers cannot 'police' or know whether people are writing fact or fiction. There are situations when fiction is a way of writing about facts, and if this provides a vehicle for avoiding some problems of personal disclosure then we should not necessarily rule it out of order.

However, the method does require a re-evaluation of what constitutes subjectivity, and the ways in which the personal can be incorporated into sociological understanding. It can be argued, within the remit proffered by postmodernism, that debates about authenticity need to move away from a duality which distinguishes between truth on the one hand and lies on the other. Truth may be less important than the shifting and fragmented identities which in a multiplicity of ways undergo constant reconstruction. Such a re-evaluation does not entirely get around the numerous difficulties that there might be, however, when practitioners find differences between personal experience and accounts they believe are 'fictional'. Perhaps one way in which such issues can be dealt with is to confront them head on, to ensure that students also critically address the issues of 'recall', of changing meanings over time, and of their own role if making their lives or experiences available to others, in order to see that 'authenticity' is itself a problematic concept in the analysis and construction of identities.

Conclusion

In this chapter we have considered existing models of learning from experience in the light of postmodern approaches to the analysis of the self and the reading and writing of lives in texts, while noting that such models often oversimplify the processes and time dimension of this kind of learning. We have sought to highlight the diversity as well as the commonality of different approaches to autobiography and personal experience to be found in practice, and what basis such models have as a starting point for practitioners. Theories of learning, ideas of what students need to learn and feminist concerns with the personal were all found to be important, and while not all practitioners mention a particular model of learning, there is clearly a belief that utilising personal experience and forms of autobiographical production provide benefits for students' learning.

Practitioners are not unquestioning or uncritical enthusiasts. On the contrary, they critically reflect on and evaluate their own experiences with these forms of teaching and learning. But they are enthusiastic about what they see as the kind of learning that can be achieved in the approach, such as the 'deep learning' of connecting ideas with experience, of relating theory to practice and understanding of self and its connection with the social. Models of learning from experience place considerable emphasis on changes that are brought about in the individual. Many practitioners, however, while arguing that personal development is something which can occur through this approach, place more emphasis on its capacity to meet traditional learning outcomes of academic programmes of study. In courses concerned with training practitioners, in for example community development, social work, education or health care, the personal development model can more easily be allied with ideas of improving practice. In the sociological context, the primary aim remains the understanding of social structures and processes.

The practical application of autobiographical approaches to teaching and learning in sociology revealed some of the issues for teachers which writers such as Boud, Keogh and Walker (1985) have highlighted as part of the process of learning from experience. These include dealing with emotions and related questions of ethics and what we have called safety for teachers and learners alike. Some teachers are doubtful about their own ability to manage the consequences. We have surmised that this is a limitation on the use of these methods, particularly for individual teachers who do not have the benefit of a supportive team of colleagues. Certainly, other ethical issues concerning privacy, the degree to which students are obliged to do autobiographical work, and the degree of personal information offered by staff also require attention.

Despite the strength of the argument for the place of autobiography and learning from experience in adult education and the social sciences, it seems to be used only by a minority of teachers. One reason for this may be that it remains a demanding and resource-expensive approach. It requires a good deal of negotiation with students, for many of whom it will appear to be an unfamiliar approach. Furthermore, the boundaries, expectations and requirements for assessment need clear articulation. We referred at the beginning of this paper to C. Wright Mills's injunction to social researchers to 'capture what you experience and sort it out' (Mills, 1970: 216). Extending this process into the social science classroom is clearly no easy matter, but we believe that attempts to do so, in enabling students to 'grasp biography and history and the relations between the two within society' (Mills, 1970: 12) and thence to develop students' sociological imaginations, are well worth the effort.

Acknowledgement

We would like to acknowlege, with thanks, the input into the project by Dr Helen Powell. Her work and ideas were important to the development of this chapter.

Notes

1.   This concept involves the idea that understanding and ability to integrate ideas is key to effective and quality learning, to be contrasted with surface learning of associated didactic teaching and high content modules (see Ramsden, 1992; Gibbs, 1981).

2.   To take the practice of one of us (BH) as an example here: with all dissertation work a strong emphasis on the value of research diary; and in teaching qualitative methods it is stressed that this is an important tool that makes explicit the role of the researcher in the research process and reflection as an element of credibility.

7 Using Computer-assisted Assessment in Sociology

VICTOR JUPP, LEE BARRON AND ALAN HESLINGTON

Introduction

This chapter outlines the main forms of computer-assisted assessment, their use in a sociology undergraduate programme, and raises issues regarding their use. It is based on experiences of developing and implementing such forms of assessment in some areas of the sociology curriculum at the University of Northumbria at Newcastle. This was part of a wider project on assessment managed from Bath Spa University College and funded under HEFCE's Fund for the Development of Teaching and Learning.

What is CAA?

Computer assisted assessment refers to any form of assessment where the delivery and or the marking of assessments is carried out by computer technology. Two main forms will be described here. These are:

- *Computer-based assessment*

This usually involves students interacting with a PC and responding to questions which are asked on screen. Students are informed of their success by using a mouse or keyboard to answer a question or battery of questions and may also be given feedback in relation to their answer(s). Students may use stand-alone PCS, networked PCS or the world-wide web. One advantage is that the technology allows the use of multimedia. Graphics, sound, animation and video can all be used to good effect. As well as enhancing the presentation of questions this can also help in constructing questions to test higher order skills.

- *Paper-based assessment*

In this case students respond to a paper-based multiple choice examination paper by making horizontal marks through the option of their choice in much the same way that a National Lottery ticket is marked. Question papers usually contain a series of options, often labelled A to E, one of which is the correct response, and a typical question paper would contain around fifty to sixty questions to be answered in one hour. Answer sheets are processed using an optical character reader (OCR) or an optical mark reader (OMR) which read and mark the papers and produce detailed reports and question analysis. In this sense the assessment is computer assisted, as the computer is only part of the assessment process.

Apart from its use in assessment computer technology is also employed in teaching and learning in various ways. For example:

- Computer Assisted Instruction (CAI)
- Computer Based Training (CBT)
- Computer Managed Learning (CML)
- Computer Assisted Learning (CAL)

In their differing ways these are all characterised by the use of computer technology to deliver a body of knowledge, often broken down into sub-units or modules of study. This allows learners to work and progress at their own pace, often as an individual working independently and at a distance; and sometimes providing feedback to students at designated milestones in their studies.

The Value of Assessment to Learning

Although this chapter is primarily about assessment it does not recognise a clear divide between learning by students on the one hand and assessment by staff on the other. A basic assumption is that assessment should be integral to a course of study rather than something that is 'tacked on' to the end. Assessment should be closely related to aims and outcomes and, moreover, it can be a form of learning in its own right that helps the student achieve aims and objectives.

Computer technology is a useful means of providing a 'once-and-for-all' assessment (sometimes referred to as summative assessment). It can also be used to assess students at the same time as providing almost instantaneous qualitative feedback on answers to particular questions and on overall performance on a test (sometimes referred to as formative assessment). Many studies have shown that early feedback (corrective and supportive) is the most effective form of assessment. The ways in which feedback on individual questions and on batteries of questions is illustrated later in this chapter by reference to the 'Principles of Social Inquiry' course at the University of Northumbria and its use of Computer Assisted Sociology Tutorials, or CAST.

The Value of Assessment to Teaching

Assessment should play an integral part in teaching (including lectures, seminars, readings, etc.), its evaluation and in the quality loop which leads back to changes and improvements in the curriculum and how it is delivered. Statistics generated by computer-assisted methods can play a valuable role in this process. For example, at an elementary level statistics can be produced on:

- The percentage of students who get a particular question correct.
- The mean and standard deviation of marks for a group of students.
- The distribution of student answers across options for any given question.
- The incorrect answer which is chosen most frequently by students.
- The intercorrelations between success on clusters of questions on the same topic.
- The intercorrelations between success on clusters of questions on different topics.
- The reliability and discrimination of questions.

The careful examination of such statistics can provide an important and early assessment – not just of the individual student – but also of the curriculum and its delivery. Put at its simplest, if a small minority of students get questions on one area of knowledge wrong then there is every chance that the failure is the result of their lack of understanding. If a large majority of students get questions on one area of knowledge wrong then there is every chance that the fault lies somewhere in the curriculum and/or the ways in which it is delivered.

This is illustrated later in the chapter by reference to statistical reports generated by OMR examinations in 'Principles of Social Inquiry' which identified that the mean score for the group as a whole was low for certain areas of knowledge. This led the tutor to examine why this was the case and to put in place additional support materials for these areas for the next cohort.

The main theme of this chapter so far has been that there is value in a close integration between, on the one hand, assessment and on the other hand, teaching, learning, evaluation, quality assurance and curriculum development. Such integration is not dependent on the use of CAA but it is greatly enhanced by it in terms of the ways in which it provides feedback to student learning and staff curriculum delivery, and the speed at which it does this.

Matching Uses and Types of Assessment

As mentioned CAA can be used in relation to both summative and formative assessment. The primary aim of summative assessment is to make judgements regarding the level of understanding of a body of knowledge on the part of individual students. This usually takes place at the end of the unit of study or at periodic intervals as the student progresses through sub-units. Typically, summative assessment results in a pass or fail designation, a grading or the assignment of a percentage score. The primary aim of formative assessment is to help the student improve, hopefully to the point at which all learning outcomes are achieved. Such assessment is continuous and is supported by feedback to the student, usually in the form of words. Scores indicating overall performance may also be offered. Feedback is especially effective when qualitative feedback and numerical scores are closely related and support each other.

Of the two methods of CAA mentioned the computer-based interactive tutorials are most appropriate to formative assessment insofar as they typically provide the student with immediate feedback after the student has answered a question. This allows the student to pause and digest text which outlines why particular choices are correct or incorrect. They can also provide an overall score and feedback relating to overall performance. Students can repeat tests – having learned from a previous attempt – and seek to improve on their score up until the point at which they are satisfied with their level of attainment. Computer-based assessment can also be used for summative purposes but, of course, students are only permitted to take the test once. Also its use with large groups is restricted by the IT facilities available in an institution. Multiple sittings of an examination are possible but it may be necessary to produce multiple tests, which can negate savings in staff time, and would require rigorous checks to ensure that the tests were of the same degree of difficulty.

Paper-based examinations that are marked by some form of optical reading are much more suitable for summative assessment with very large groups of students. They do not provide instant feedback – which, of course is not so important with summative feedback – but they can be taken in conventional examination situations as they are not dependent on the use of a computer terminal. Within the Principles of Social Inquiry course, a formative assessment consisting of a mock examination using OMR was conducted within the course seminar programme. Detailed feedback was provided on each question with small student groups, assessing the students progress up to that point of the course and providing students with sufficient information to direct their learning in preparation for the final summative assessment, again using OMR.

The Use of OMR: A Case Study

At the University of Northumbria at Newcastle, students studying the unit 'Principles of Social Inquiry' are assessed at the end of semester one by an objective test that is marked using Optical Mark Recognition. Within this assessment format, students are required to answer fifty MCQs, each with five responses, in one hour.

Question Analysis

One of the major benefits of computerising objective tests is the ability to analyse individual questions. Reports produced by OMR software enable the examiner to identify which questions were not answered well by students. This is often due to poorly worded or ambiguous questions.

OMR software allows a detailed analysis of individual questions. We now consider student response to three questions taken from the 'Principles of Social Inquiry' specimen examination paper. The three examples below show the questions, possible responses and a table showing the percentage of students opting for each possible response.

Discrimination is a statistical measure of how well a question discriminates between strong and weak students. This is calculated by comparing student scores for that question with their scores with the test overall. A discrimination of 0.4 or above is generally considered to be an indication of a good question. Other statistics including mean and standard deviation are also generated, but not shown.

Finally a graph gives a breakdown of the percentage of students who answered the question correctly by ability groups, ranked according to their overall performance in the test. The first column represents the percentage of correct responses for the top fifth of students, the second column represents the next fifth of students, etc.

Example 1

Which one of the following theoretical approaches is typically associated with the use of Social Surveys?

A)   Positivism
B)   Ethnomethodology
C)   Symbolic Interactionism
D)   Marxism
E)   Feminism

Student Response

A   B   C   D   E

71% 21% 5%   1%   1%

Discrimination 0.58   Correct Answer A

For this question the majority of students (71 per cent) chose the correct response. Although three of the distracters attracted very little attention the question still shows good discrimination.

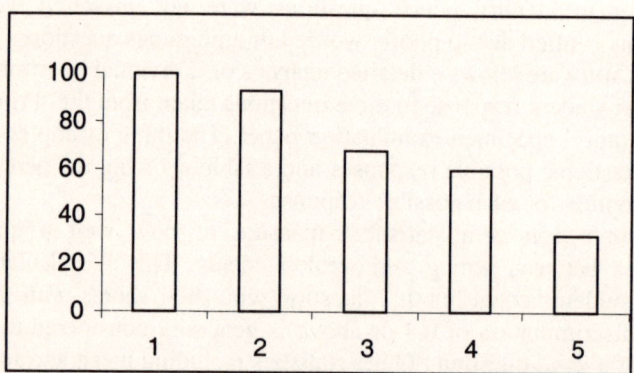

The graph indicates that all of the top fifth of students answered this question correctly, followed by 96 per cent of the second fifth etc. A graph that shows 'steps' descending from left to right is a simple visual indication of a good question.

Example 2

Which of the following is a problem associated with participant observation?

A) Interview bias
B) Artificiality
C) Control effects
D) Over-involvement
E) Naturalism

Student Response

  A   B   C   D   E

  18% 19% 9% 45% 6%

Discrimination 0.55   Correct Answer D

Here the responses are more evenly spread out, and it can be seen that only 45 per cent of students have answered this question correctly, with other responses shared between the distracters. The discrimination of 0.55 suggests however, that this is a good question.

This is supported by the shape of the graph, where the responses by ranked ability groupings are 80 per cent, 65 per cent, 37 per cent, 25 per cent and 19 per cent.

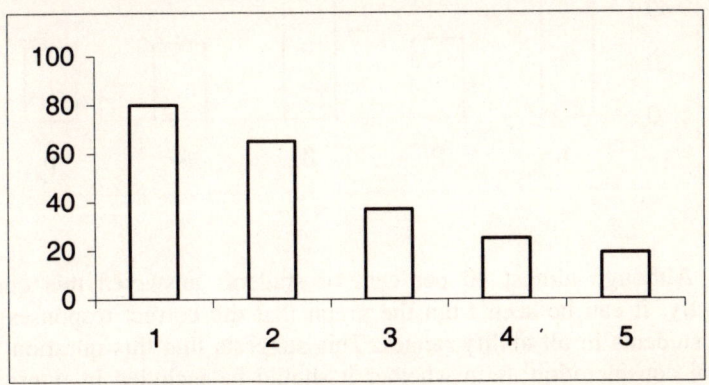

Example 3

What are 'reforms as experiments' also known as?

A)   Controlled experiments
B)   Random experiments
C)   Evaluation research
D)   Laboratory-type experiments
E)   Ethnography

Student Response

A	B	C	D	E
20%	16%	37%	14%	11%

Discrimination 0.15   Correct Answer C

At first glance the responses to this question do not seem too dissimilar to those for Example 2 – 37 per cent answering correctly and other responses evenly shared out. The discrimination of 0.15 suggests however, that this is not a good question.

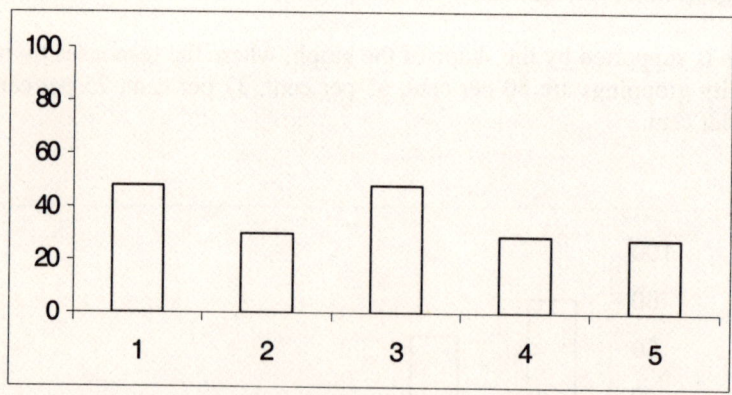

Although almost 40 per cent of students answered this question correctly, it can be seen from the graph that the correct responses came from students in all ability ranges. This suggests that this question needs careful consideration as to whether it should be included in future tests.

This detailed question analysis would not be possible for hand marked objective tests.

A good account of the use of OMR can be found in 'OMR as CAA – experiences at Loughborough University' by Myles Danson, in *Computer Assisted Assessment in Higher Education*.

Comments from Staff

Trials with OMR at UNN have also involved the divisions of Psychology and Economics. Although we are primarily concerned with the use of CAA for Sociology, it is worth noting some of the comments made by staff from these subject areas:

- 'results reached us very quickly'.
- 'it allowed us to see which areas proved difficult to students'.
- 'using OMR has proved a great success'.
- 'writing good MCQs is not easy!'.

With increasing student numbers and a move to semesterisation CAA and the use of OMR means that more students are being assessed more frequently. OMR can mark over one hundred papers in an hour, allowing lecturing staff to devote more time to research, course design, lecture preparation etc. In using OMR for the 'Principles of Social Inquiry' course, the benefits included:

- ability to examine a whole unit of study;
- avoidance of 'question spotting';
- contribution to variety in assessment methods;
- savings in staff time;
- results produced quickly;
- reliability in marking (no errors as the outcome of marker fatigue);
- anonymity of marking;
- objectivity in marking;
- administrative savings;
- detailed reporting enables the evaluation of the curriculum and its delivery;
- the establishment of a clear benchmarking threshold;
- reduced examination time for students;
- production of a good spread of marks.

The Use of Interactive Tutorials for Formative Assessment

The Division of Sociology at the University of Northumbria at Newcastle has considerable experience in the use of Computer Assisted Assessment. A series of formative tests for students studying research methods were introduced in 1990 for the unit 'Principles of Social Inquiry'. These tests were popular with students and were of a high calibre, but quickly became outdated due to limited presentation (black and white screen), and complicated syntax required by the user in order to run them. These tests were transferred to the Question Mark for Windows format. The transfer of the tests to the Question Mark format enabled the use of colour, sound and graphics – important factors for student motivation. It also allowed for more detailed and varied feedback after each question and at the end of each test.

The tests were re-named CAST (Computer Assisted Sociology Tutorial). Further tests were written, and the software currently comprises eleven tests of approximately fifteen questions each:

- types of data;
- language of social research;
- experimental method;
- social survey;
- history of official data;
- official statistics;
- ethnography – basic commitments;
- ethnography – data collection;
- descriptive statistics;
- research using text;
- types of theory/method.

CAST has been produced in a CD Rom format that can be installed onto the hard drive of a PC in less than a minute. CAST will run from Windows NT, Windows 95 and above, and will run from some lower specification machines, but there may be a reduction in the quality of the graphics and the speed of response of the software.

The CAST tutorials are built into the programme so that they form an integral part of the learning process. Students are directed to tutorials as part of their learning programme outlined in the course handbook:

Week beginning	Lecture	Readings	Seminar	CAST tutorial
11.10.99	Experiment-ation	Milligram & Honey et al pp 48–56	Designing a questionnaire	Experimental Method
18.10.99	Survey Populations	Maclean & Bolton et al pp 34–47	Observing work	Social Survey
25.10.99	Measuring Society	Durkheim & Black et al pp 85–118	Observing Work	Official Statistics

Students access the tutorials by choosing the CAST icon that is loaded onto the desktop of the PC monitor during installation. They are then presented with a push button main menu screen from which to choose the tutorial that they wish to work on. On completion of each tutorial students are returned to the main menu screen. They can then choose to work on another tutorial or exit from CAST.

An 'Example Questions' button gives examples of question types. It is recommended that students who are not confident in using a PC look at these to familiarise themselves with the software before starting a tutorial.

The first screen of each tutorial gives an indication of content. Students can then choose to start the tutorial or they can return to the main menu screen. CAST uses four question types – multiple choice, multiple response, selection and push-button True/False questions.

Question Mark for Windows allows three other question types – numeric, text match and hot-spot (in which the user drags a cursor to an area of the screen), although these are not used in CAST.

Multiple Choice Questions

A multiple choice type question consists of the question (stem), the correct answer (key) and a number of incorrect options (distracters).

In this example, taken from the ethnography: basic commitments tutorial, the student has chosen the answer 'positivism'. Choosing 'Continue' would then result in the answer being marked and feedback would be provided.

True/False Questions

A True/False question consists of the question and push-button responses – similar to the buttons on the main menu screen. This is effectively a multiple choice question with only one distracter, but it does allow for variation in presentation of questions.

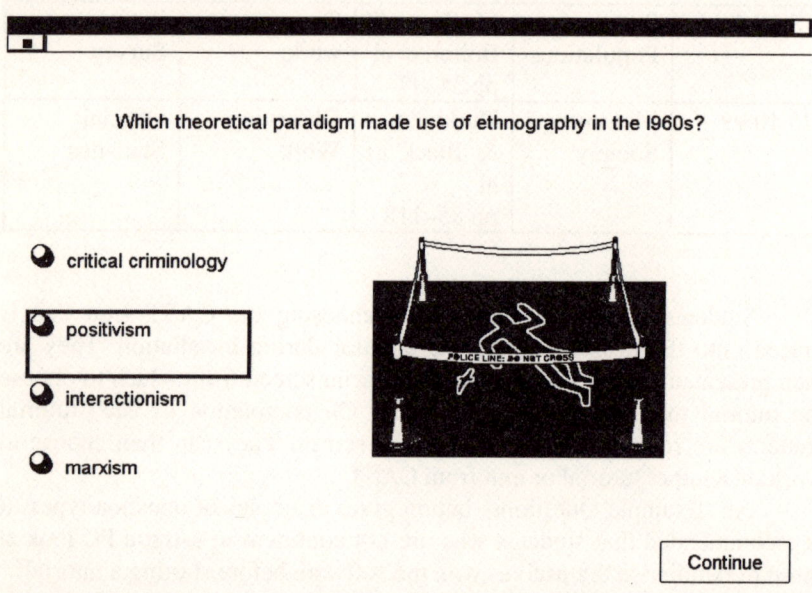

Which theoretical paradigm made use of ethnography in the I960s?

- critical criminology
- **positivism**
- interactionism
- marxism

Continue

Selection Questions

Selection questions consist of a question or statement and then a choice of possible answers from a scroll down list.

Here the question is taken from the descriptive statistics tutorial, and the student has assigned gender as nominal data, salary as ratio data, exam grade as ordinal data, and is yet to decide what best describes temperature.

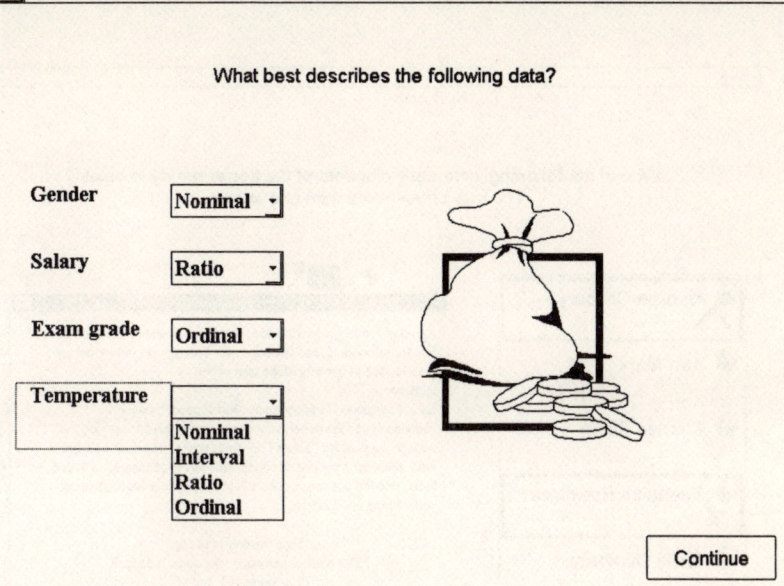

What best describes the following data?

Gender	Nominal ▾
Salary	Ratio ▾
Exam grade	Ordinal ▾
Temperature	▾
	Nominal
	Interval
	Ratio
	Ordinal

Continue

Multiple Response Questions

A multiple response question is similar to multiple choice, except that there is more than one correct response. It is important that students are made aware of this in the wording of the question. In the example above, taken from the social survey tutorial, the student has chosen the options Cadbury and Rowntree. This question has been 'marked' by the software, which identifies Cadbury as an incorrect response, Rowntree as a correct response and Booth as the correct answer not chosen by the student.

The end of question feedback can be used to explain why a particular response is incorrect or to give further information.

For multiple choice and True/False questions this feedback can be specific to the response chosen by the student. For multiple response and selection questions the feedback is standard, due to the large number of possible combinations of responses.

We refer to CAST as tutorials rather than tests because the emphasis is on learning rather than assessment. The immediate feedback provided after each question ensures that students can learn from their mistakes.

Students are encouraged to re-take the tutorials as often as they wish until they reach what they consider to be a satisfactory standard.

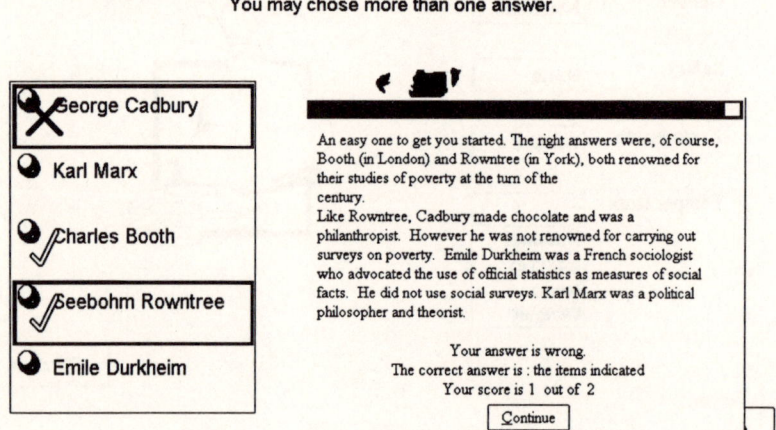

Who of the following were early pioneers of the social survey in Britain? You may chose more than one answer.

George Cadbury ✗

Karl Marx

Charles Booth ✓

Seebohm Rowntree ✓

Emile Durkheim

An easy one to get you started. The right answers were, of course, Booth (in London) and Rowntree (in York), both renowned for their studies of poverty at the turn of the century.
Like Rowntree, Cadbury made chocolate and was a philanthropist. However he was not renowned for carrying out surveys on poverty. Emile Durkheim was a French sociologist who advocated the use of official statistics as measures of social facts. He did not use social surveys. Karl Marx was a political philosopher and theorist.

Your answer is wrong.
The correct answer is : the items indicated
Your score is 1 out of 2

Continue

End of Tutorial Feedback

At the end of each tutorial the student is provided with further feedback. This feedback varies depending upon the score obtained, and will include suggestions of further readings.

'*User name: John Smith*
Score: 68%
Date: 22/11/99

A good mark, but don't be complacent if you know that you can do better.

In analysing data it is essential that you fully understand the statistical concepts that you are dealing with (there are many statistical packages that will do the calculations for you).

You might like to read Chapter 8 and 9 in Sapford and Jupp's "Statistical Analysis", or other appropriate text.

This feedback can vary, depending on the score obtained by the student. The benefits found from the use of Computer Assisted Sociology Tutorials on the Principles of Social Inquiry course include:

- provides immediate and detailed feedback;
- appropriate for independent learning and distance learning;
- students can work at their own pace;
- students can evaluate their own performances;
- students can identify areas of weakness;
- staff can evaluate student progress;
- staff can evaluate curriculum and its delivery.

'Principles of Social Inquiry' and CAST

At this point it is worth evaluating the technical aspects outlined above with some accounts of the actual practice and experience of using CAA at the University of Northumbria at Newcastle. The most telling indication of the value of computerised assessment comes from the impressions of the students who have used it and the effects the system had on their academic progress. Within the 'Principles of Social Inquiry' course, CAST tutorials replaced the previous computerised tutorial system, which was effective, but involved highly specific access procedures, which many students would find difficult and often choose not to use as a result. However, CAST is a far more attractive and user-friendly system and had an immediate impact upon students taking the course.

The course comprises a set of lectures, each exploring an aspect of research methodology and the theoretical underpinnings of the various methods and a series of classroom based seminars. The purpose of the seminars is to illustrate such theory using a set of practical exercises. In addition, students are directed to other resources, including CAST. The teaching of the seminars involves conducting a mock OMR examination and it is worth discussing examples arising from this examination which highlight the educational benefits of CAA, and CAST in particular.

The mock examination is a paper-based test consisting of twenty-five MCQs to be completed in thirty minutes within a seminar session. Although the papers are marked using the OMR system, students are given photocopies of their papers which they mark in accordance with the given feedback in the subsequent seminar session. The purpose of the mock examination is three-fold. It assesses the Principles of Social Inquiry course informally, allowing students the opportunity to bring the course together before the revision period begins. The students are allowed to practice what is an unfamiliar assessment format, so that they are comfortable with the system of assessment in the formal examination; and the mock examination allowed tutors and technical staff the opportunity to use the OMR system and test its capabilities.

In terms of outcomes the effects of CAST were dramatic. To demonstrate this it is worth citing the case of one particular student. This student scored 34 per cent in the mock examination, a score which would have constituted a failing mark in a formal examination. The CAST system was introduced for this 1998 student cohort in the weeks leading up to the formal examination of the course. This failing student used the tutorials extensively throughout the revision period prior to the examination and on taking the examination scored 74 per cent. This mark constituted a 40 per cent increase which took the student from a failing mark in the mock examination to a very good pass mark in a six week period. On discussing this mark, the jubilant student felt that the CAST tutorials had focussed their reading and revision and had enabled them to grasp what until the mock examination the student had felt had been overwhelming and confusing terminology. The student strongly emphasised that without CAST she would have continued to struggle with the subject. This is supported by the findings of Dr. Tony Bates from the University of British Columbia, whose research showed that students taught by CD-Rom attained better examination results than students who had attended face-to-face lectures. Speaking at the first annual conference of the Institute for Learning and Teaching, in York, Dr. Bates stated that: 'students learning from a CD-Rom had 30 per cent better recall after three months compared with a control group attending conventional lectures' (*The Higher*, 20\6\00: 56).

The following academic year raised another student who had struggled in the mock examination and had used CAST to help with revision. The student in question pinned a note on the first year notice board at the beginning of the 1999 academic year, which read:

> Attention all first years
> A tip: Principles of Social Inquiry.
> If the tutorials are available – start now!
> They are invaluable!!!

This incident highlights the perceived benefit of a student using CAST to prepare for the OMR examination. The mock examination feedback seminars afforded tutors the opportunity to witness at first hand the direct effects of CAST in terms of helping students to draw material together and to provide a solid grounding for revision. These sessions also afforded the tutor the opportunity to urge students who had not yet begun to use the CAST system to do so, to discuss the nature of the tutorials and stress the benefits to be gained from extensively making use of them. As the above examples show, CAST can assist students who initially have a weak grasp of the subject to not only gain a passing grade, but to attain excellent marks. In the last academic year, the CAST software was further improved and more students made use of it as the following comments demonstrate.

Student Feedback on CAST

The success of CAST and its introduction into the sociology teaching programme is ultimately best articulated by the thoughts of the users of the system itself. What follows is a number of comments made by 'Principles of Social Inquiry' students about their feelings on using the CAST software and how it helped them understand the subject of research methodology.

These comments provide an excellent qualitative assessment of the educational benefits of CAST tutorials and the system of examination using OMR:

> This is my first attempt on CAST tutorials and I obviously need a lot more practice!! However, I have found this to be great fun so I will be back very soon!!!!

> This is a good way of acquiring a foundation from which to study the topic more fully.

> I find these tutorials a great help. I plan to write down the answers, revise and return to CAST to see how much I've learned. I'm so glad they are here to practice on. When I get a high score it really gives me confidence.

> Very useful, especially in determining weak areas to go away and work on.

> I found this method very helpful and useful revision.

> This was my first try at CAST. I found this very informative and a good way for students to chart their progress.

Very useful, I wish all units had these tutorials!

I have just completed the experimental method tutorial for the third time and my mark is getting higher.

[The tutorials] prepared me for the question wording on the [examination] paper

CAST changed my life! It was a godsend

Such comments speak volumes in articulating the impact of CAST upon the teaching of Principles of Social Inquiry and stress factors such as confidence building, the clarification of terminology and an effective means of examination preparation as the clear benefits of using CAST in conjunction with both set and wider readings.

Quantitative evidence revealed that students on this course expressed favourable opinions on CAS and OMR. Students agreed that navigation through the CAST system was uncomplicated; that the instructions were straightforward to follow and questions easy to understand. The end of question feedback and end of test feedback was reported as being good; students felt that they had control of learning and found CAST enjoyable to use; and crucially, felt that CAST prepared them well for the final examination. With regard to the OMR paper-based examination, students felt that the instructions were clear, the questions covered the content of the syllabus, and the assessment method was preferable to more traditional methods of assessment such as essay writing.

Staff Feedback on CAA

As well as student feedback on role of CAA within higher education institutions, the thoughts of teaching staff must also be addressed. This is a summary of comments made from staff.

The key points to emerge relate to both pedagogic and pragmatic issues. Tutors report that CAA allows the tutor a more structured style of course delivery which can pinpoint areas of factual knowledge and to spread it across a whole course thus making sure students pick up the main points the tutor wishes to convey and what they need to know. CAA provides a solution to the staff-student ratio taking the pressure away from Level One marking, time which can be devoted to more rigorous Level Two and Level Three marking. CAA allows results to reach tutors very quickly and provides tutors with the opportunity to see which areas proved too difficult or too easy for students.

Problems and Issues

There is little evidence that sociologists in the UK are enthusiastic about CAA. However, as indicated in the preceding sections, the benefits to be gained from the use of CAA can be considerable, although they do need to vary according to whether one uses interactive tutorials or some form of optical marking and whether they are used for summative or formative assessment. There are, however, problems and issues that need to be addressed. These range from the practical to the epistemological and include:

- 'The use of certain forms of CAA, especially interactive tutorials, assumes that there is adequate access to PCs. Not all institutions can guarantee this'.

- 'The use of CAA is disadvantageous to those who have computer phobia or who experience computer anxiety'.

- 'CAA is not appropriate to the nature of knowledge and of learning in higher education'.

This general criticism can come in a number of forms such as:

- 'It is not appropriate for higher levels or orders of knowledge'.
- 'It is mechanistic and reductionist'.
- 'It doesn't test analytical skills'.
- 'It doesn't encourage and reward critical thinking'.
- 'It doesn't assess aspects of writing, expression and communication'.
- 'It doesn't assess the ability to marshall an argument'.
- 'It encourages education based on recall rather than understanding'.

In noting these objections, it is essential to point out that we do not argue that CAA should replace traditional modes of teaching and assessment. Rather, the stated advantages of CAA suggest that it complements other forms of course delivery and assessment. In addressing specific issues, CAA can be strongly defended.

In terms of computer access and institutions which cannot provide widespread IT facilities then it cannot be disputed that there would be difficulties in providing widespread teaching provision utilising CAA. There is a problem with courses such as 'Principles of Social Inquiry' which have in excess of two hundred students. Access to computer laboratories is limited, but if students use the CAST tutorials consistently from the beginning of the course rather than leaving them until the assessment period is looming, then this issue is less problematic. However, a more efficient solution would be to install CAST onto a network or make it Web-based, actions that would greatly enhance availability.

An example of a simple web-based Sociology multiple choice test, 'Know Your Society', has been produced by University College, Northampton and is available at:

http://www.northampton.ac.uk/ass/soc/nws/html/know_uk.html.

With regard to issues such as students being disadvantaged because of computer phobia, CAST is specifically designed to remove this. As stated the previous computerised tutorial system did involve a more formal access procedure which students would sometimes have difficulty with. As a result, some students simply would not use the tutorials. However, CAST, using Question Mark can be accessed with the simple double click on the CAST icon on the desktop. Example questions familiarise students with question and feedback from users suggests that the software is easy to navigate.

More serious issues involve the effectiveness of CAA with regard to the nature of learning; namely the views that CAA is mechanistic and reductionist, that it is does not test analytical skills or encourage and reward critical thinking. In addressing these issues, it must be noted that typically, Level One student assessment is descriptive in nature, with evaluation and critical analysis expected in Levels Two and Level Three. With regard to the issue that CAA encourages education based on recall rather than understanding, this can be challenged using examples from CAST which illustrate that student responses are not simply based upon recall. For example, if we take the following questions drawn from the Ethnography CAST tutorial:

Which one of the following is NOT a commitment of ethnography?

A) Verstehen
B) Multiple Perspectives
C) Naturalism
D) Search for causality

To choose the correct answer D, which refers not to ethnography, which emphasises the qualitative, interpretative theoretical approach but belongs to the hypothetico-deductive quantitative tradition. In order to answer correctly students must understand what the commitments of ethnography are to recognise why the search for causality is not typically one of its underlying principles. Similarly with the question:

Which of the following forms of data collection is NOT typically associated with ethnography?

A) Analysis of documents
B) Life history interviews
C) Structured interviews
D) Participant observation

Again, to answer correctly, in this case option C, the student must understand the differentiation between qualitative and quantitative methodological approaches. Therefore, to answer correctly on both CAST tutorials and the paper-based OMR examination, which contains many questions in the format outlined above; students require understanding of the topics and cannot rely simply upon recall.

While it is true that CAA does not assess aspects of writing, expression and communication, it does exists alongside courses whose assessment formats are based on these principles. The nature of 'Principles of Social Inquiry' is to provide a solid foundation of knowledge that will be the basis of Level Two research methods courses that will use written assessments. In addition to the OMR assessment, Level One students are undertaking courses that are being assessed by essays and examinations that require two or more essays. CAA is just one of many assessment formats which will enrich the assessment experience and test different skills.

The charge that CAA is reductionist can be countered by the fact that CAST, in providing a framework and focus for learning, is primarily a springboard for further reading and not a substitute for it. The 'Principles of Social Inquiry' course contains a range of readings which reflect classic examples of different methodologies, for example Durkheim's 'Suicide' illustrating the use of official statistics. These readings are assessed by sets of questions within the final examination. Similarly, at the end of every CAST tutorial feedback instructions provide recommended readings which are essential for successful examination results. As the following student feedback demonstrates:

I do find these sessions very informative, especially now it is coming up to my mock exam. Finding time to do them is the hard part. It is a good way of learning what you need to know and also being able to understand where you need to improve in certain areas. Reading Jupp's book (Methods in Criminological Research) and revising from these sessions will be my main priority before the mock exam.

I think the tutorials are very beneficial especially after reading a particular text then giving yourself little tests to make sure you have understood.

Some of the terminology in general is confusing so identifying it on the [CAST] tutorials sometimes proves challenging. Nevertheless, CAST continues to reinforce my notes taken on lectures and also personal notes.

The charge that CAA is not appropriate for higher levels or orders of knowledge is not entirely disputed. There are areas of knowledge which do not lend themselves to assessment using CAA the most obvious of which is the teaching of sociological theory. To break down arguments such as those proposed for example by classical sociologists such as Emile Durkheim in 'Suicide' or Max Weber in 'Economy and Society' which cover such detailed and diverse subjects such as the nature of positivism and the varied social causes of suicide or the differing conceptions of rationality and authority would be reductionist and against the spirit of theoretical engagement.

Similarly, the debate concerning difficult and often ambiguous postmodern theorists such as Jean-Francois Lyotard or Jean Baudrillard, who actively resist definitions within their writings, and to articulate the critical reactions against such theory could not adequately be assessed using CAST tutorials or OMR type examinations. Such topics ideally require written assessments that encourage critical engagement and detailed analysis. To reduce such higher level knowledge to short definitional categories that would serve as the basis for CAST tutorials would be too limiting and ultimately too simplistic for higher level theorization.

However, that is not to say that developments could not be made to enhance critical engagement within CAA assessments and there are specific ways in which such shortcomings could be overcome. One way of using CAA to specifically engage students in descriptive, critical and analytical thinking about a range of key theoretical issues without forfeiting their complexity and their interrelationships with other theoretical concepts would be to provide students with a piece of unseen text, and then ask questions relating to this.

The examples below are taken from the Graduate Record Examinations (GRE) Sociology test, which asked five questions relating to the following text:

'Two sociologists have analyzed the extent to which there has been "male flight" from computer work and whether such work has become "resegregated" and "ghettoized". They summarized some of their study's findings as follows:

We have examined in detail several hypotheses culled from the literature on the processes of occupational resegregation and ghettoization. Our results are not consistent with the predictions of these hypotheses. The data indicate that during a period of rapid feminization of computer work, the earnings of computer specialists did not decline relative to those of the labour force as a whole. Men left computer work more often than did women, but they were also more likely than women to enter computer work from other technical fields. Men were more likely to exit computer work for related lines of work, while women were more likely to leave the labour force entirely. When relevant factors were controlled, men were less likely to leave computer work than were women. Thus, the mid career attrition of men did not contribute to the feminization of computer work; on the contrary, women were more likely to leave computer work than men with similar characteristics.

Moreover, the particular mechanisms held to be responsible for men leaving computer work do not account for the variation in male exit rates. The variation in men's earnings relative to their peers in the labour force was not a reliable predictor of men's attrition. This finding is inconsistent with the prediction that declines in earnings are responsible for male flight from feniinizing occupations. Nor did feminization per se provoke male flight. In those specialities where women's entry was most pronounced, male exits were not statistically different than in other specialities.

The disproportionate attrition of women from computer work is paralleled by a decline in the proportion of women pursuing bachelor's degrees in fields leading to careers in computer work.

1.   One of the clear implications of the study is that

A)   an increase in the percentage of women in an occupation does not necessarily lead to male flight.
B)   high-technology work is increasingly attractive to women.
C)   promotional opportunities have become rather blind to gender.
D)   corporate policies have become more favourable toward women in technical positions.
E)   there is a consistent tendency for technical work to become feminized.

2.   Which of the following statements concerning the study and work satisfaction is accurate?

A)   The study suggests that men are less satisfied with computer work than are women.
B)   The study suggests that women are less satisfied with computer work than are men.
C)   The study suggests that when women are not satisfied with their work, they leave the labour force.
D)   The study suggests that work satisfaction contributes to people leaving their jobs but does not cause people to leave their jobs.
E)   The study presents no evidence regarding work satisfaction.

(Further details of GRE tests can be found at:

http://www.gre.org/codelst.html)

Of course, preparing such assessments is time consuming, but sophisticated software exists that enable banks of questions to be stored for use in later years.

Conclusion

The use of CAA within the various departments at the University of Northumbria at Newcastle have shown that it is an excellent tool for providing core skills and knowledge for First Level students, and as such enriches the student assessment experience. CAA is simply one of many assessment techniques now in operation within the university, it is not intended to replace assessments based upon extended writing (essays, written examinations etc.). Nor is it being suggested that CAA should be used throughout all year groups. With regard to the 'Principles of Social Inquiry' course, CAA has given students a full grounding in all aspects of social research, a grounding which is essential for studies at Level Two. CAA allows tutors to extensively teach and assess a full range of topics that other courses based on more traditional forms of assessment cannot do.

The CAA experience at the University of Northumbria at Newcastle has demonstrated the advantages of computerised assessment in terms of course provision, examination performance, and perhaps most crucially of all, the students themselves have assessed the CAA programme favourably in terms of the system providing them with a strong educational output.

Acknowledgement

The GRE materials on pages 119 and 120 are reprinted by permission of Educational Testing Service, the copyright owner. Permission to reprint GRE materials does not constitute review or endorsement by Educational Testing Service of this publication as a whole or of any other testing information it may contain.

8 Social Relations and Intellectual Evaluation in Self and Peer Assessment

JENNIFER PLATT, REBECCA WILLISON, TIM REED, HELEN
GRAHAM, JOHN ABRAHAM AND RUTH WOODFIELD

Introduction

'Self-assessment' is a concept less current among sociologists than it is
among educationists, where it has some vogue. In the educational literature,
the term has been used to refer to a gamut of practices ranging from critical
evaluation by students of their work in progress, to provision by students of
the official assessment mark for completed work. There are senses in which
these are equivalent, but also senses in which they are very different, the
first conventionally appearing as 'teaching' or 'learning' – formative
assessment – and the second as 'examining' – summative assessment. The
new data presented in this paper cover only a limited range of practices,
nearer to the summative end of the spectrum, though some of what they
reveal is suggestive about a wider range of possibilities. Much of the vogue
of the idea is more for the formative than the summative end of the
spectrum. Much of the literature on 'self-assessment' is written by
enthusiasts for the idea; self-assessment is perhaps sufficiently deviant from
standard practice across universities to select mainly those with
commitment to such approaches to try it and write about it – though it is
possible that many others practice some parts of what they write about
without calling it 'self-assessment', or writing about their experience. This
chapter is written from a more pragmatic point of view, which assumes that
it is intrinsically neither attractive nor beyond the pale. The focus is both on
presenting the data, and on considering their implications for practice.

Practices of 'self-assessment' may be used for a variety of aims,
some instrumental within the course (e.g. to encourage students to reflect
on their work so that they will improve it, to promote internalisation of

faculty marking standards) and some terminal (e.g. to equip students with skills they will need to apply after graduation, to provide a mark which will be used for grading). It is not always clear whether such aims as student empowerment are chosen for either instrumental or terminal reasons; sometimes they seem to be treated as intrinsically desirable, rather than valued for their consequences. Here we assume that, whatever other values may be held, the key ones in relation to assessment practices are those of good learning and accurate evaluation. The question of the relation between ends and means is crucial; however, an ideal intellectual fit between ends and means does not in itself ensure that a system will work well in practice. There are also other issues, of a kind we are familiar with as sociologists – for instance student motivation, or institutional constraints – which affect what happens in practice, and many organisational details can influence the outcomes; some of these factors will be examined.

The term 'self-assessment' has been used both for literal *self-*assessment – individuals assessing their own work – and peer assessment – assessing the work of other students; the work assessed has sometimes been group work, and the assessment of it may be made by individual students separately or they may work in groups. If it is peer assessment, it may be of work by known individuals, perhaps present at the time, or by anonymous individuals, and the assessment may be done publicly or privately from those assessed. All these distinctions affect how the assessment is likely to be done, and they also have consequences for who is in a position to learn what from the process. We draw attention to the implications of some such differences in the analysis below.

Review of the Literature

It would misrepresent our work to imply that it arose from or was based on the literature; it arose from our routinely developed practice, and the issues we thought of in relation to that when given the opportunity to look at it critically. It was only later that we learned something about the literature produced by those for whom teaching and assessment are central research concerns. The function, therefore, of a review of the literature here is to provide a context to which what we found can be related rather than to show where our work comes from. This is not a complete review of relevant material, but one which concentrates on the most recent, well-known and influential work in Britain.

David Boud is recognised as a leading figure in this field, and a central concern of his is represented by his book title *Enhancing Learning Through Self-Assessment*. He sees the defining characteristic of self-assessment as 'the involvement of students in identifying standards and /or criteria to apply to their work and making judgments about the extent to which they have met those criteria and standards' (1997: 12), and it is clear that his emphasis is on the first, formative, part of this process, which he sees as going with a commitment to the goals of creating independent and autonomous learners. His examples are drawn mainly from engineering, law and education. He lists work he has identified on self-assessment as used in different fields, and there is only one example for sociology, from the US in 1980 (1997: 51–2). However, he reviews work which compares student self-ratings with teachers' ratings, and reports that students tend to mark for effort where teachers mark for product, and that better students tend to mark themselves down while worse ones tend to mark themselves up; more 'accurate' marks are given by students in scientific subjects. He argues that if self-assessment is to be used summatively the marks given need to be acceptable to teachers, and suggests an elaborate set of criteria which would need to be met if they were used for an official grade.

John Cowan is another prominent author in this field, and he places a special emphasis on self-assessment as a skill which students need to learn in order to practise it in later life in professional decision-making. He stresses the importance of learning how to learn rather than just acquiring subject knowledge, and of 'deep' learning, and sees a need to be self-critical of ones own learning processes to achieve these goals; in his experience self-monitoring leads to a continual effort to improve (Cowan 1998). We may note, however, that two of his own case studies that he presents are of a group of students in civil engineering who were self-selected volunteers for this method of teaching, and of mature students taking an Open University course on 'Project Judgment and Decision Making'. These might well be somewhat unrepresentative of the general run of students even in the same fields in their motivation and learning styles. The concern is more with formative reflection on the learning process than on assessment. George and Cowan (1999) provide a rich discussion of ways in which assessment can affect learning, making a strong case for evaluating existing assessment practices from that point of view; the emphasis is not on assessment as a mechanism for accreditation, but as part of the learning process.

Peter Knight (2000) offers some valuable thoughts about the relation between learning and assessment, blurring the boundary between them. He points out that if the summative assessment process is planned as part of the teaching, and related well to the teaching and learning objectives, it may serve formative ends; ideally, learning to the test then becomes desirable, not a weakness to be criticised. He argues that summative assessment must be seen to be fair and reliable, and is better separated from formative goals to avoid confusion; however, not all worthwhile learning objectives can conveniently be assessed by appropriate summative methods, so those have to be dealt with by formative processes. He thus sets limits to the summative use of self-assessment, while maintaining that its formative use can be very helpful.

Sally Brown and Peter Knight (1994) place self-assessment in the context of a discussion of assessment in general. They too see self-assessment as encouraging autonomous learning, and giving ownership and empowerment to students, and contrast this with other forms of assessment which encourage students to engage in 'cue-seeking' behaviour oriented to exams as such rather than to learning. However, they recognise problems, such as the mutual award of high or low marks, which can arise with peer assessment, especially if it is used for grading (1994: 59–64). Nonetheless, they see discussion of potential marks as an educative process, and suggest that skills can be improved by briefing on the criteria to use, and by building up experience of the process (1994: 105).

Thus the general impression is that, while 'self-assessment' is warmly advocated, the advocacy is much warmer in relation to formative than to summative goals – at the same time as there is a valuable emphasis on the formative implications of summative practices. What actually happens when it is in some way used summatively appears to have been less explored than the contribution to valued formative goals.

No published work apart from that cited by Boud has been identified which relates specifically to sociology, and little that is related to the social sciences more broadly. It is not clear why most of those who have written in this area should teach in the fields of education, science and technology, or professional training, but caution seems appropriate in assuming that their methods and findings would be equally applicable in sociology; both the fields and the types of student they attract may differ in ways that have consequences for the effects of the same practices. The typical sociology undergraduate is not a mature practitioner with an established professional identity in the field, and for much of the time is not working in areas where there are firmly accepted right answers or direct practical tests of application. The work reported here deals with sociology undergraduates, and with the summative aspects of some routine and experimental practices used with them.

Research Methods

Data are presented drawn from experience at the University of Sussex, mainly collected in the course of normal teaching, though some special features were added to that for research purposes. In addition, colleagues at other institutions have kindly helped by submitting some of the materials used at Sussex to groups at their own institutions, which provides a basis for comparisons which help to interpret the Sussex material.

It is not known how typical Sussex students are of Sociology students nationally. They tend to be drawn from the South-East, and the Sussex course presents itself as more interdisciplinary than many elsewhere; in the relevant cohorts the standard offer level for admission was BBB at A level, though there have also been some students admitted with lower grades, and noticeable numbers of mature students from local Access courses. As elsewhere, there has been a fairly low proportion of men, and most students are in the age range 18–22; the typical cohort is of 50–60 students. The relative homogeneity of these groups, and their modest size, mean that potentially interesting comparisons rapidly run into such small numbers that little can be made of them. However, it seems likely that some key findings do not depend on such characteristics of the samples used.

There have been three points in the Sussex sociology student career at which some element of 'self-assessment' (mostly peer assessment) has been used; these, and the methods used in collecting data on them, are described below.

First-year Induction Session

The first point is an 'induction' session held for first year students half way through their first term, which took place for the first time in 1998. This included several activities, the relevant one of which was about essay writing. An essay by a former student on a course they were then taking had been circulated in advance, and they were asked to read it and think how they would mark it; in the group induction meeting, the initial marks were collected, students were formed into small groups to discuss their marks and agree one as a group, and all the marks were collected and discussed by the course convenor, who also explained why he had marked the essay as he did. Inevitably, not all the students who attended the session had in fact read the essay and marked it in advance, so for some the group discussion was combined with thinking seriously about the matter for the first time. Attendance was good, but probably skewed towards more committed and conscientious students; as usual on these occasions, mature women students were prominent. This meeting was just before the submission of the first essay was due, and its purpose was to help with understanding what was expected in a university essay, and to sensitise students to factors which they should try to take into account as they wrote. The exercise was generally felt to have been a helpful one, though we have no hard data on its success in improving the essay-writing process. Data was collected on the marks given, and on some of the discussion that took place. Five students, who had given the essay different marks, were interviewed soon after the meeting (by a recent Sussex graduate who was also taking them for discussion classes on the course in question).

The 'self-assessment' here was public but doubly anonymous peer marking.

Principles of Sociological Analysis Presentations

There is an established first-year course, Principles of Sociological Analysis, where, in the summer term, students work independently in groups to make a critical evaluation of a chosen sociological book. The aim of this, apart from its specific intellectual content, is to encourage work independent of faculty input, and to cultivate group work and presentational skills. The groups initially form themselves, so there is naturally a tendency for them to consist of friends, but any student not signed up in that way is allocated to a group. At the end of the course each group makes a presentation on its work to the entire year-group. This presentation is marked by members of faculty, and the mark contributes to the total mark for the course. The students are given in advance the choice of whether that mark, whatever it may be, should be apportioned among the members of their group equally, or should be weighted by individual contribution; at the end, if they have opted for weighting they are asked to provide the weightings for their individual members. There is, thus, a potential element of group 'self-assessment' of the contribution that each member has made. This provision was introduced in order to allow for the likely variation in individual contributions, thus preventing free riders and recognising above-average contributions to the total outcome.[1] It was perhaps also assumed that the existence of such a provision would make free riders less likely.

In the summer term of 1999 we had a participant observer at work who tried to investigate how student groups addressed the issue, and what the consequences were for participation and behaviour of the existence of the mark-sharing provision. We also collected data for research purposes on the presentations day about how students would mark the presentations. There were 10 groups, each of 6 students; five made their presentations in the morning, and five in the afternoon. In the morning, markers were simply asked to give each presentation (including their own, though not all did this) a mark out of 100, and to make any comments they wished in the (very small) space provided; not everyone made comments – and some made comments but gave no mark. In the afternoon, specific criteria were suggested; the sheet provided questions such as 'Was the presentation well organised? Did it flow smoothly?', with space for comments in reply. (There were no official marking criteria laid down.) Students were instructed not to discuss their marks with anyone else, but it was observed that some of them did so; it was also observed that only some of them appeared to take the exercise seriously.

The 'self-assessment' which contributed to the official mark was public, non-anonymous peer assessment by small groups of individuals; that which was done only for research purposes was private, anonymous assessment of non-anonymous groups of peers by individuals.

Sociological Research Methods: Project Presentations

There is also a long-standing provision that, in the third year, each student is required at the end of the spring term to make a presentation to the whole year-group about the empirical project they carry out. The initial intention of this was merely to give students further practice in making presentations, to encourage them to learn from the projects of their colleagues too, and to give a deadline before the final submission date by which they needed to have organised their data and ideas so that last-minute work was discouraged. In recent years, however, attendance became poor, so it was decided that the presentations should be marked, and the mark should count towards the Finals mark for the course; it now has a weight of 20 per cent, while the report on the project, submitted later, counts for 80 per cent. The primary aim of this was nonetheless a formative one, to increase the chances of our original aims being met. Attendance has improved strikingly, and the occasion is now taken very seriously.

The project presentations are individual, and include no formal element of self-assessment. In 1999, however, we added an experimental peer assessment exercise; the results did not contribute towards the marks, but they are still of some interest in throwing light on what can happen in such situations. The presentations took place over two days, and students were required to attend the whole day on which their own presentation was scheduled. Each was given a list of the day's presentations, and asked to mark every presentation they attended – including their own, to preserve anonymity.[2] A list of the official criteria that faculty would use to mark the presentations had been circulated in advance for student guidance; these included points on both form and content. It did not allocate specific numbers of marks to different features of the presentations. Students were instructed to mark independently, and not to discuss their marks with anyone else, and the mark sheets were collected at each break. Some wrote notes on the mark sheets of how they characterised particular presentations, although they were not asked to do this, while others just handed in a numerical mark.

On the first day they were instructed to follow the official criteria, while on the second they were instructed to use whatever criteria they themselves felt appropriate (and encouraged to comment on what those were). Students allocated themselves to a day by signing on a list, and they were not told in advance that there would be a difference between the marking instructions for the two days. Since different students made presentations and marked them on the two days the comparison between the two treatments is hardly a strict experimental one, but it was felt that it could nonetheless be of some interest. We cannot be sure that students had not divided themselves between the days in some unidentified non-random way. (We do know that, for timetable reasons, a high proportion of those on the first day were all taking the same option, on Deviance – but this is extremely popular, and does not obviously select a particular type of student.) The gender balance was different between the days, so that comparisons between the sexes can only be made for the first; the first day was attended by 14 women and 8 men, while the second had 20 women and only one man. We do not know if there was any communication between the students on the first day and those on the second which might have affected the latter.

The 'self-assessment' here was private, anonymous assessment of non-anonymous peers, and included a small but often unidentified element of individual self-assessment.

Our analysis of the results rests both on the marks given, and on some participant observation carried out by a research assistant (another recent graduate) to find out how students viewed the exercise and carried it out. Timetabling problems meant that not every student actually attended for the whole time they should formally have done, so some mark lists are incomplete. (Two only turned up a few minutes before their own presentations were scheduled; some others were sufficiently annoyed by this to mark them down for that reason.[3]) A few students submitted lists with one or two marks missing. That may reflect unwillingness to mark their own presentations, or difficulty in evaluating a particular presentation – or may just indicate a trip to the loo. All marks provided have been used, except that for measures of the *range* used by individual markers those whose marks omitted more than two presentations have not been included.

For these presentations, we also have comparative material from elsewhere.[4] A video recording was made of six of the presentations, three by men and three by women, which had received official marks ranging from 40 to 75, and this was sent out with instructions which provided the official marking criteria and asked students to mark each presentation first by the official criteria and then by their own. (It must be noted that seeing a presentation shown on a not very professional video is not the same as being present at the live occasion, though we cannot know if any features of that difference affected the marks.) In response, data have been received from 11 graduate students in Sociology[5] at the University of Plymouth ('Plymouth'), 35 undergraduates at the University College of Ripon and York St John ('Ripon')[6] and 17 Sociology undergraduates from University College Northampton ('Northants'). Neither of the former two groups consisted solely of third-year Sociology undergraduates, so in that sense they were not precisely comparable with the Sussex students; any differences from those lend themselves to interpretation, but cannot be treated simply as if they were between students who were and were not personally acquainted with the presenters. However, that interpretation would seem more plausible to the extent that they differ from Sussex students in the same direction. Assessment by these other groups is doubly anonymous peer assessment.

Findings

Induction

The tutor who originally marked the essay used in this exercise had given it 60 per cent. The 24 individual marks submitted by students had a mean of 59 per cent, and ranged from 40 to 70; the eight group marks arrived at during the meeting had a mean of 57 per cent, with a range of 45–65. Thus the students collectively evaluated the essay very much as the tutor did and, when deviating noticeably from that, did so by more often by marking lower. The process of group discussion cut down on deviations from the mean, though it did not lead to convergence on the tutor's mark; students remained harsher critics. It would be interesting to see if they remained such if the marking were done after they had submitted their first essays and had them marked.

The interviews revealed that, for example, a student who gave the essay only 40 per cent had very high expectations of academic work and of himself; one who gave it 68 per cent had correspondingly lower expectations, and said she would have been pleased to have written that essay herself, though she felt after the general discussion that her mark had been too high. These comments suggest that students with varying expectations of themselves would in the same way tend to evaluate their own work differently. Two different marking strategies had been used, though the criteria used sound broadly similar; some marked by dividing the essay into parts, while others read it as a whole. It is not clear whether this made a difference to the marks arrived at. All agreed that it was easy to criticise anonymous work when the author was known not to be present, and that it would be much harder to be objective with friends or people they knew.

Principles of Sociological Analysis

In practice, experience over the years of the group allocation of marks on this course has hardly worked out as intended. Groups working together have seldom opted for potentially uneven weighting of marks, and when they have done so they have in the past always, in the event, chosen to give every member the same mark – even though separately they admit that contributions have actually been very uneven, perhaps even in some cases negligible.[7]

The participant observer reported that all the students she spoke to said that they had divided the marks evenly among their group, although actual contributions had not been equal. However, the participant observation did not give the whole picture, since in that year for the first time two groups of students did give uneven marks, in both cases only by giving no marks to a member who had never taken any part in their preparations. Against this background we cannot, unfortunately, report on how different types of contribution have been assessed, or what weighting criteria have been used. However, an important observation made was that it appeared that those regarded as 'freeloaders', whether or not they had been marked down, tended to be people who had been allocated later to the self-constituted groups of friends which formed the nucleus of most groups. A variety of social reasons could be suggested for this – for instance: outsiders were socially excluded from the group, or normally met its members less, and so could only make a lesser contribution; outsiders were less attached to the university community, and so felt less commitment to their studies; outsiders did as much work as anyone else, but were perceived as doing less because this was less salient to other members, or was of a kind which their shared norms valued less... We do not have data on which, if any, of these applied, but their possibility should make one uneasy about some potential reasons for evaluating the contributions made as unequal.

At the time when the groups were asked to make the decision on how to distribute their marks the work was not far forward and they did not realise the problems that could occur; many students said that with hindsight they would like to have chosen the option of dividing the marks unevenly. However, it is far from certain that they actually would have made an uneven division in the end, since most also said that it would be socially awkward, and the opportunity would probably never be used. (One suggested that perhaps this could be got round by having a secret vote on how to do it.) Complete absence, as in the cases mentioned above, presumably eases the social stress involved, but that does not help with less clear-cut situations.

For the presentations, the tutors' agreed marks ranged from 55 per cent to 72 per cent, a range of 17. Student marks ranged from 45 to 100, with the longest range used being 35 and the shortest only seven marks. For every group but one the mean student mark was higher than the tutors' mark, the difference ranging from 2 to 10; the mean tutor mark was 61, and the mean student mark 66. There was despite that a fair consensus on rank order, but with differences of more than two ranks for two groups; it is not clear what distinguished those from the others. Groups which marked themselves on average gave themselves 5 marks above the mean mark from other students. It is interesting to note that groups which did *not* mark themselves were those marked lowest by the others. Was this a way of avoiding the issue?

The qualitative comments written in for the morning presentations were thin, but on what they covered have a fair resemblance to those suggested on the marking sheet for the afternoon. It is not surprising that aspects of how interesting/lively/engaging to the audience the presentation was are frequently mentioned, while comments which imply independent knowledge of the book the presentation was about and the adequacy of the presentation in relation to that were much less prominent – though there were some comments on, for example, whether the presenters showed knowledge and understanding of the book.

Sociological Research Methods: Project

For the presentations on this course, a number of students expressed unease about their ability to mark satisfactorily. One wrote on her form 'I don't feel qualified to do this', and several said to the observer that they were not sure how to relate the qualities of a presentation to a mark. They also said that this problem was particularly felt at the beginning of the day, though later on after seeing and marking a number of presentations they gained confidence – and would have liked to go back and change some of their earlier marks. In addition, some felt they could not give full attention to others' presentations until they had done their own, and so until then 'just wrote down anything'. Both those factors mean that the marks given later in the day should perhaps be treated as a fuller and more informed expression of their views, though we have not here distinguished earlier from later marks.

It is immediately striking that different students marked in very different ways, so that much is concealed by averaging, though we sometimes have averaged. In particular, some used only a very narrow range of marks, while others marking the same presentations used a much wider range.

Table 8.1. Ranges of Marks given* by Sussex Students to Project Presentations (official criteria)

Mark														
42														X
43														X
44														X
45														X
46														X
47														X
48														X
49											X			X
50									X		X			X
51									X		X			X
52							X	X	X	X	X			X
53							X	X	X	X	X			X
54							X	X	X	X	X			X
55							X	X	X	X	X	X		X
56							X	X	X	X	X	X		X
57							X	X	X	X	X	X		X
58	X						X	X	X	X	X	X	X	X
59	X			X		X	X	X	X	X	X	X	X	X
60	X	X		X	X	X	X	X	X	X	X	X	X	X
61	X	X		X	X	X	X	X	X	X	X	X	X	X
62	X	X	X	X	X	X	X	X	X	X	X	X	X	X
63	X	X	X	X	X	X	X	X	X	X	X	X	X	X
64	X	X	X	X	X	X	X	X	X	X	X	X	X	X
65	X	X	X	X	X	X	X	X	X	X	X	X	X	X
66		X	X	X	X	X		X	X		X	X	X	X
67		X	X	X	X	X			X		X	X	X	X
68			X	X	X	X			X		X	X	X	X
69			X	X	X	X			X			X	X	X
70			X		X	X			X			X	X	X
71									X			X	X	X
72									X			X	X	X
73									X			X	X	
74												X	X	
75												X	X	
76												X		
77												X		
78												X		
79												X		
80												X		
81												X		
82												X		
83												X		
84												X		
85												X		

* Each column represents one student marker, and shows the top and bottom of their marking range; they did not necessarily use all the mark points between the extremes.

The extremes of length of range of marks used, among those students who marked all, or all but one, of the same presentations, are marks of from 58 to 64 or 60 to 67, and 42 to 72, for the day when official criteria were to be used, and from 63 to 68 and 50 to 89 for the day when their own criteria were to be used. (Faculty mark ranges were 44–75 and 20–75 for the two days.)

Many markers concentrated their marks in the 60s. It seems highly likely that different students were using the same numerical marks with different meanings: a 61 from someone whose lowest mark was 60 does not seem to convey the same meaning as a 61 from someone else whose lowest mark was 48 and highest mark 73, or who used only a higher or lower range. If they were not using the same marks with different meanings, they were showing high levels of disagreement in their marks. [8]

When the official criteria were used, the average marks given by those using long ranges (operationally defined as a difference of 16 or more between highest and lowest mark) are *higher* than the marks of those using a short range for every presentation when their average mark is 65 or above, and *lower* for every presentation when their average mark is 59 or below; this reflects the very strong tendency for the short ranges to be concentrated in the middle 60s. When students used their own criteria, the same general pattern applies. [9]

Why did some students use such a narrow range? Our qualitative data may throw some light on this. Many students said they found it hard to assess people they knew, and also that they gave everyone fairly good marks, because of fellow feeling and a preference to do as they would be done by. They also said that if they knew someone was a dedicated student they gave a good mark even if the presentation was not good. These factors in combination could well lead to the compression of marks into the 2.1 range. However, there is no way in which we can distinguish between narrow or high mark ranges used because the students really could not see how to discriminate more, or thought all the presentations were good, and ones where social factors were distorting their underlying 'real' assessments.

On average, faculty marked lower than students and, as one might expect, the average difference between them was greater (7.8 as compared with 4.95) when the students were invited to use their own criteria. Given that faculty used relatively long mark ranges, it might be expected that the average difference between their marks and the student ones would be greater where students used only a short range, but that was not the case.

However, the range of differences varied considerably, with a few cases where faculty marked higher, and it could be more interesting to identify what it was that led to greater or lesser differences. The cases where faculty marked much lower than students *did* have distinct characteristics, which mean that the difference between the marks can almost certainly not be imputed to the criteria to be used; they are ones where the student was characterised by faculty as making bad decisions about what material to cover, rather than covering it badly. Our participant observer reported that those she talked to who had been using their own criteria generally said that they marked only on the basis of presentational skills and rapport with the audience. It seems likely that students were less clear about their model of an adequate presentation, and paid more relative attention to purely presentational factors than to errors[10] or omissions of content.

Women students marked slightly but very consistently more favourably when using the official criteria; for every individual marked except one male presenter, the women's mark is higher or (3 cases) equal. The average marks given by the women (on the 'official criteria' day, the only one when enough men were present for comparison) were, thus, slightly higher for both male and female presenters than those given by men; the men concur in giving themselves a lower average mark. Both groups are, on this point, in agreement with the faculty. We note that this does not confirm earlier findings about men's tendency to rate themselves relatively highly (cf. Beyer, 1999).

Comparisons by age of marker show that on the day when the official criteria were used younger markers both male and female marked more generously than older ones. When markers used their own criteria there was not such a clear-cut pattern, and in 4 cases there was a reverse age gradient. It is not easy to interpret the difference between the two days. Perhaps it simply suggests that when people can choose their own criteria there is more diversity, because they have not been socialised into any shared standards? It could also suggest that older students are, by virtue of their age and experience, closer in their judgements to members of faculty and therefore have a better grasp of what the official criteria imply.[11]

Comparison of the averages of the Plymouth, Ripon and Northants marks using the official criteria with the Sussex student ones shows that Sussex marks were always higher than or equal to the highest mark by other groups. They gave every presenter a mark in the 2.1 range, while Plymouth and Ripon markers gave that class to only two of the presentations (those marked highest by Sussex faculty); Northants markers also gave it to another one. It might have been expected that the Plymouth group would, as the ones most similar in experience and role to the faculty, have given the marks most similar to theirs, but their marks were not closer than those of the Ripon students.

Table 8.2 Average Mark given to Different Videoed Presentations (official criteria)

Presentation:	1	2	3	4	5	6
Sussex faculty: agreed mark[12]	*55*	*75*	*44*	*55*	*40*	*59*
Sussex faculty	55	71	45	57	38	63
Sussex undergraduates	61	67	61	62	-	-
Ripon undergraduates	57	65	51	49	51	66
Northants undergraduates	61	61	55	55	-	-
Plymouth graduate students	57	67	50	50	53	70

The Sussex students as a group used a very short range of marks, only equalled by Northants. Although there was fair consensus among all the groups on rank order, Sussex faculty marked their highest candidate higher, and the lowest one lower, than did the students, and so had the widest range of marks – but two groups of the non-Sussex students used ranges much closer to those of the faculty. One may speculate that the similarity of the range used by the Northants students is connected with the fact that they too were all sociology undergraduates, though if so there is no indication whether that would owe more to commonality of intellectual experience or to feelings of social solidarity. However, it would be unwise to make too much of ranges when there are only four or six cases on which to base them.

Table 8.3 looked at the length of range between average group marks; it may be more meaningful to look at the ranges of marks used by individuals, as Table 8.4 does. This leaves Northants as the group most similar to Sussex, but brings out the extent to which many individual Sussex students used shorter ranges than all the other groups. Worth exploring for future research could be the possibility that there are two different styles of coping with the task, which lead to the use of short and long mark ranges; if so, what are the factors which lead students to fall into one or the other camp?

Table 8.3 Length of Ranges* of Average Presentation Marks given (official criteria)

	first 4 video cases	6 video cases
Sussex faculty	26	33
Sussex undergraduates	6	
Ripon undergraduates	16	17
Northants undergraduates	6	
Plymouth graduate students	17	20

* i.e. difference between highest and lowest mark given.

Table 8.4 Average Length of Ranges of Presentation Marks used by Individuals (official criteria)

	first 4 video cases	6 video cases
Sussex faculty	26	34
Sussex undergraduates	5	-
Ripon undergraduates	22	28
Northants undergraduates	12	-
Plymouth graduate students	21	27

Conclusion

The data presented show that there were both group variations in marking, and pronounced individual variation within groups. Unfortunately we cannot throw much light on the sources of individual variation, though this would seem important to understanding the processes involved and thus to improving practice. (A tempting hypothesis would be that higher marks, and shorter ranges of marks, are given where social pressures are felt most strongly.) It is clear that the social pressures can be strong in face to face relationships, and that de facto anonymity (but not necessarily mere privacy of the marking) can make a considerable difference. (Another tempting hypothesis is that presentations will always evoke social relations to some extent, even when what is seen is a video of strangers, while the dry impersonality of an essay without any image of its writer is less likely to do so.) Any realistic use of *peer* assessment, especially if it contributes to summative grading, must take such factors into account.

There are perhaps ways to diminish, if not wholly to overcome, the effects, although we have not yet tried them. The most obvious possibilities are practice in marking, with discussion of the issues it raises, and the provision of marking instructions which indicate how many points should be allowed under each subhead. If self-assessment were intended to train students to evaluate their own work or their peers' 'correctly', in the sense of agreeing with the marks given by members of faculty, the student/faculty discrepancies we have found make it evident that many of them would need more training than our students were given; that gives a message potentially relevant to formative as well as summative self-assessment. Where contribution to group work is being marked, such instructions might provide for records to be kept (meetings attended, tasks completed, deadlines met...) which could provide an objective basis for a final decision, though this would not help much with less objectively clear contributions such as the merit of the ideas put forward.

But unless training would deal with the social pressures, to treat it as the answer to the problems is implicitly to assume that the marks given represent the students' 'real' evaluations of the merits of the work of others that they are marking. But that may not be so; one cannot tell from inspection of the marks given to what extent they reveal intellectual evaluations, and to what extent they reveal social pressures. It seems that they are much more likely to represent intellectual evaluations when the markers do not know the authors of the work, and/or do know that they are not present or will not know of their evaluations. But when they do represent the 'real' evaluations, it is still possible that essentially the same evaluations will not be represented in the same way by numerical marks awarded, and that is an area where training would obviously be relevant again.

No such devices could, however, overcome the basic fact that undergraduate students will always (one hopes) know less about the field than do the faculty teaching them, so it might be more appropriate to confine the areas where student marks count summatively to those, such as the effectiveness of presentations for an audience, where students are equally or better qualified to judge. Thus the appropriateness of such training would vary with the kind of work to be marked. There is reason to believe that in our presentation cases tutors laid greater stress than students did on the adequacy of the *content* of what was said, rather than just more or less entertaining performances, even though the public criteria mentioned both. But that is not at all surprising when tutors will necessarily have much greater independent knowledge of the contents of the books on which presentations are given, or general knowledge of research methods, than is expected of students evaluating presentations by their colleagues; the presentation in its own right may be all that students can have access to. The same may not apply when they are marking essays for a course where at least in principle they have done the same reading and had the same teaching as any other student taking the course – though in practice there will surely be considerable variation, and still few are likely to have read as much as the tutor. When students do evaluate, what criteria do they use? And what criteria *can* they use? These problems will arise whether it is their own work or that of peers that they are evaluating, and whether the evaluation is made for formative or for summative purposes.

We do not know what our students derived formatively from the practices examined – though the colleagues who provided our comparative data report that the exercise led to some valuable discussions among their students – so this chapter cannot contribute to that discussion. We can, however, suggest that, at least in groups more typical of sociology undergraduates than those reported on in the wider literature, the social pressures in peer marking, and the intellectual problems in marking ones own or other students' work, merit more attention.

Notes

1   Gledhill and Smith (1996: 19) have shown how students may feel that it is impossible for faculty markers to avoid giving unearned marks to free riders, and for that reason be unhappy about group work. However, our experience does not support their perception of peer assessment as an answer to the problem.

2   However, they were invited to identify themselves on the sheet if they did not mind doing so, so that literal *self*-assessments could be compared with assessments by others; such a small minority did so that no results are reported.

3   The one woman and one man involved should not have submitted marks, or should have submitted them only for the last two or three presentations. Unfortunately inspection of the mark sheets reveals that, although the man did not submit any marks, the woman submitted one at least for the whole afternoon, for most of which she was not present. Since we do not know which her mark sheet is, we cannot eliminate it from the data. Fortunately, since she was only one of 14 her inappropriate marks are unlikely to make much difference to the totals.

4   The assistance of Eric Harrison, Chris Clay and Andy Pilkington in obtaining these data is acknowledged with gratitude.

5   All these postgraduates had some experience of marking undergraduate work; they had been trained to mark from written guidelines.

6   These students came from mixed social-science majors, only some Sociology.

7   Gledhill and Smith (1997: 13) show the same pattern among their students.

8   Only eight students took the option of identifying themselves – not enough to skew the overall figures. But in any case, their marks for themselves differed little from the average of those given by other students, and then not always in a positive direction. It is interesting that a majority of the men identified themselves, while only a small minority of the women did; this might be seen as showing the traditionally greater self-confidence of men – but four of the five gave themselves lower marks than the others did, so self-confidence did not take the form of unduly favourable estimation of their own performance.

9   The narrowness of many ranges of marks made comparisons of rank order impracticable, since individuals gave numbers of presentations the same mark.

10   We are embarrassed, as methods teachers, to admit that several students described samples as 'random' which certainly were not, and so lost marks for that. We did not notice other students flinching at those descriptions.

11   The anonymity of the mark sheets means that we are unable to check whether better students marked lower than weaker ones did, as the literature suggests, so we do not know what contribution that factor may have made to the results.

12   This is the mark recorded as the official one, while the next row is the average of the initial marks of the two separate markers. For Ripon students, by accident six out of 35 saw a video which only had four presentations on (not including the one that faculty marked lowest), so for them only the four cases were available. For Northants students, time only allowed for four cases to be shown, and not every student succeeded in marking the last one. For the Sussex students the same four cases are covered, since the first four came from the first day; the second day's marks were by their own criteria, and so are not comparable for the last two. Plymouth students saw all six presentations.

9 Conclusion: Reflection and Speculation

ERIC HARRISON AND ROBERT MEARS

Introduction

In this final chapter we review the activities of the *Assessment Strategies and Standards in Sociology* project. In doing so we will seek to achieve two aims. Firstly, we identify a number of key themes raised in the course of the seven contributions to this volume. Secondly, we offer some speculative remarks about future trends. The apparently disparate nature of the sub-projects, some concerned with innovation, others with improving current practice, ought not to obscure the fact that because the contributors are sociologists, broader issues have been raised by them. These are not just self contained projects. They connect with a wider agenda in which managerialism and collegialism collide and the status of the 'autonomous' university teacher is called into question.

Learning Lessons

We learned early on in the project that improving 'assessment' was not a simple matter of revising tools, just as a good sociologist would avoid thinking of 'data collection' as a simple technical exercise uninformed by theory. Once one starts thinking about assessment tools, one is led to reconsider what it is one is trying to assess. Very soon one becomes ensnared in quite fundamental questions about epistemology – the nature of the discipline, the nature of knowledge, what we think we are doing when we teach our students. Sociology as a discipline is in a very powerful position to address issues of reliability and validity of different assessment methods.

When we embarked upon this project, we initially adopted a very straightforward approach to the identification and dissemination of good practice. With hindsight, it is clear that this was naïve to say the least. Of course we had many reservations about a simple model of dissemination. As researchers in communication studies would be quick to point out, there is no straightforward relationship between message and receptor. Academic cultures are inimical to such common sense notions and individual lecturers resistant to the rhetoric of 'training'. In the course of our work we became embroiled in the changing discourses about learning and teaching between traditional and innovative methods, and the much broader debates about academic freedom and University autonomy. The project also raised a range of questions about the extent of central government interference in academic life, the boundary between individual notions of academic freedom and the role of the state in accrediting and evaluating academic provision. It seems increasingly clear that the two strands of our work are becoming more inter-related. If departments introduce more diversity in their assessment, in order to reflect their aims and their audience, this is bound to involve judgements about comparability of standards. The work by Pilkington et al and Platt et al in this volume vividly demonstrates this. If on the other hand departments are only motivated by compliance with external regulation (for instance in the form of benchmark standards), then it is still the case that conforming to these benchmarks will necessitate changes in assessment practice. Thus the project was always as much about standards as it was about strategies.

The activities reported in this collection are examples of sociologists working both to improve current and well established methods of assessment (Pilkington et al) and those that challenge us to think afresh about how either new technologies or autobiographical experience could be harnessed to improve assessment and enhance sociological learning (Jupp et al, and Harrison and Miller, respectively). The two chapters in question make the point that whereas autobiographies and new technologies are well-established and well-respected areas of research in sociology, they have made relatively little impact on teaching, learning and assessment. One of the modest aims of this collection is that in bringing together the work of several sociologists from a range of institutions, it will encourage readers to reflect and revise their practice. Five years ago a lack of innovation was identified as a problem as well as a mismatch between intentions and outcomes. Our own evidence suggests that while adoption of innovatory methods of assessment may be patchy, there has been a growing realisation that programme design must pay greater attention to the fit between curriculum aims and assessment tools.

During the two years that we spent on the project we encountered sociologists from half the departments in England, during the course of seminars, departmental workshops and at conferences. It was often reassuring to work with colleagues passionate about their discipline and keen to discuss the best ways of engaging students in sociological debates. Of course they were often a self-selected sample and we faced the obvious problem on occasion of talking only to the converted. Nevertheless, we were impressed with their willingness to share their experiences with others and their genuine curiosity about improving the reliability and validity of assessment. Many spoke of the welcome opportunity for reflecting upon teaching and learning issues. Modularity has brought a degree of fragmentation. Despite the mushrooming of teaching and learning committees and quality groups, these tend to be concerned with formal compliance and processes that satisfy internal and external audit. By contrast our activities offered a space for collective reflection and sharing of insights and practice within the context of a single discipline. We know from anonymised workshop evaluations that colleagues hugely welcomed this opportunity.

Alongside these experiences it would be misleading if we presented an unequivocally positive portrait. From the very start we encountered widespread indifference to our activities – non-response, cancelled or stillborn workshops, poor attendance at events, or on occasion a general atmosphere of 'attendance through conscription'. Those working in staff and educational development will no doubt recognise this description. We had assumed that our activities would be seized upon eagerly by our colleagues. In fact it took considerable effort and the utilisation of informal networks to get the project off the ground at all. The lukewarm response of sociologists in England to some of these teaching and learning initiatives tells us a number of things: firstly it reinforces what we know about the relative status accorded to undergraduate teaching relative to the production of research output. Some colleagues reluctantly declined to get involved, citing institutional pressure to avoid activities that could not contribute to the Research Assessment Exercise. Secondly we came up against a deeply entrenched suspicion of any projects that might herald further state interference in academic life. Many sociologists expressed the view that the whole FDTL initiative was aimed at diverting attention away from the declining unit of resource in Higher Education. Thirdly, despite our best efforts, our participants were drawn disproportionately from former polytechnics. There are a number of possible explanations for this. For a start, the institutional missions of these bodies emphasise teaching to a greater extent; in addition there is the legacy of Council for National Academic Awards (CNAA), which had embedded within public sector institutions procedures and practices which stress the explicit articulation of goals, outcomes, curriculum and assessment tools. Moreover these institutions have a higher concentration of staff receptive to 'teaching issues', either because of their career trajectories or the way they saw their job descriptions, or both. This raises intriguing questions about the segmented nature of academic labour markets to which we return later in the chapter.

Under-researched Areas

It has become apparent to us that sociological researchers have neglected some crucial areas for investigation. Despite a long-standing sociological interest in labour markets and their operation, relatively little is known about the academic labour market for sociologists. The rapid expansion of the discipline, its diffusion throughout other programmes (professional, vocational) and its contribution to new multi-disciplinary areas of interest (media studies, cultural studies, urban studies, health etc.) have all combined to make the paths into sociology teaching more variegated and career trajectories afterwards more complex. A related issue is occupational socialisation; again the discipline furnishes us with many revealing studies of how agents become nurses, doctors, accountants, lawyers etc., but very little is known about the ways in which our students make sense of a sociological education. The third area which is under-researched is our students' understanding of the discipline and how exposure to sociology succeeds or fails in transforming 'common sense' thinking. Media sociologists have been quick to alert us to the dangers of assuming that 'the audience' is always an undifferentiated mass. Despite frequent references to the potential of sociological thinking to be personally transformative, we lack any firm data to confirm this. Even the large sub-discipline of the sociology of education has focused overwhelmingly on schooling. Consequently the discipline has generated very little research on its own impact within university settings, both upon individuals and on groups of students. There is therefore a curious lacuna when it comes to theorising the impact of sociology, the taught discipline, on not just hundreds of thousands of undergraduates but also schoolchildren. This contrasts markedly with the current concern about the value of sociological research for its 'users and beneficiaries'.

Looking Forward

The Disenchantment of the Discipline?

Sociologists should be particularly sensitised to the powerful rationalising tendencies within late modern societies. To that extent, performance indicators, quality audit, calls for transparency and the movement towards evidence-based practice are simply an inevitable consequence of the drive towards greater predictability and calculability in all spheres of public life. Therefore, it seems unlikely that these processes will be reversed. The language of accountability and transparency will dominate debates for some time to come. The monitoring and evaluation of teaching quality through revised systems of academic review have already become entrenched in the culture of institutions.

Why should this have been the case, given the enormous hostility which exists to such regimes of regulation? One uncomfortable answer may be that the transformation of the higher education sector in the last decade makes such a regime necessary and even inevitable. Thirty years ago there existed an 'invisible college' in University sociology. There were relatively few departments, the discipline was less diverse in terms of its paradigms, and many practising academics had shared a common undergraduate experience, either at the University of London, Leicester or half a dozen other institutions offering the subject at the time. By the 1990s the discipline was being taught in a hundred institutions in the UK. Sociology had become more diverse in terms of its student intake as the HE system approached participation rates of 40 per cent, its content had not only expanded in size but no longer appeared to have a consistent and shared 'core'; the epistemological battles of the 1970s left the discipline in less agreement about its purpose, its method and its assumptions. Some celebrated this diversity; others mourned the loss of certainty. At the same time sociology staff were no longer emerging exclusively from sociology departments and courses in a small number of institutions. This exacerbated the breakdown of the previous consensus which underpinned assessment practice. In short, from the 1960s onwards, sociology became more diverse in terms of its location, its audience and its practitioners.

This has of course happened to most disciplines during the expansion periods of the late twentieth century, but we would argue that sociology has experienced this in an exaggerated form because of its late arrival in academe and its subsequent rapid growth in popularity. This led to questions such as 'who is teaching sociology?', 'what can we legitimately expect from different types of student?' and most worryingly, 'what constitutes a good sociology education?'.

Those sociologists who have turned their attention to the analysis of Universities in late modernity have characterised the current landscape in higher education as the late arrival of Fordism or indeed the emergence of the post-Fordist University. Why? The drive towards standardised systems of credit rating, modularisation, the imposition of 'quality control' mechanisms and the massification of higher education are explained in terms of these wider social processes (see Parker and Jary, 1998). This is not the place to do justice to these arguments. While we recognise much that is familiar in this portrait, we believe that we should avoid characterising these trends as either the ultimate triumph of a centralising state, or the victory of postmodern arguments which emphasise a decentralising, consumer-led, market fragmented university system.

Accounts of any social phenomenon which privilege centralizing tendencies run the risk of neglecting equally powerful counter-processes. Centrifugal and centripetal forces are always and everywhere part of the same structure. As Elias (1994) reminds us when writing about state formation processes, centralising tendencies will trigger resistance and such counter tendencies will, in turn, provoke further bursts of centralisation. It would be a mistake to assume that one set of tendencies will triumph over the other. Recent experiences in the world of University regulation remind us of the importance of these observations. For example, the proposals for QAA-approved lists of external examiners were withdrawn when it became clear that universities would not tolerate such an imposition. Subsequently, when the QAA established subject benchmark panels, it was to the professional bodies representing academic disciplines that they turned. These examples demonstrate the limited power of the QAA to force through plans seen as unpopular or unworkable. Their continuing attempts to involve academics and their organisations in the operationalization and implementation of regulatory policy demonstrates both the limits of 'state power' and the need for the QAA to retain a degree of legitimacy within Universities. There are also pockets of resistance and continuing opportunities for 'regulatory capture'. As sociologists, we need a critique of the developing power balances between university and state.

The Future for the Subject Centre

From a disparate range of discrete projects, under the umbrella of FDTL and TLTP initiatives, has emerged a new discipline-based approach to the enhancement of teaching and learning in higher education. From the middle of 2000, 24 subject centres were established, each representing a single discipline or a cluster of cognate disciplines. At the heart of this development was recognition by HEFCE that its previous emphasis on generic pedagogy had failed to deliver significant improvements in the classroom. This appeared to be an overdue recognition of the continued importance of 'academic tribes and territories' (Becher, 1989). In addition to these centres, the Council established a single 'generic' teaching centre largely to deal with IT issues and to co-ordinate particular thematic initiatives. All the centres were to be located within specific departments known to have a track record of excellence and/or innovation in their discipline, and all were to report to the Learning and Teaching Support Network (LTSN) housed at the newly created Institute for Learning and Teaching (ILT). On paper at least it appeared that the academic community had succeeded in imposing its own model of self-regulation in this area.

Given that the sociological discipline has been charged with enhancing and developing its own practice, what now should be on the agenda for our subject centre based at Birmingham? Drawing on our experience and those of the contributors to this book, we offer some possible directions in which the centre might develop its work. Inevitably our concern with assessment and standards convinces us that these are the most pressing issues we face. We concur with Broadfoot's observations about the emergence of 'curssessment' and believe that any reconsideration of what undergraduate sociology students should be able to do will inevitably impact upon the way in which they are assessed. This means that the steps we have already taken to raise the profile of assessment issues need to be carried forward and developed further. This needs to happen with regard to both strands of our work, namely in terms both of assessment strategies and also assessment standards. By strategies here we mean two things: firstly that decisions about assessment instruments and the specific tasks which comprise them should not be taken in isolation from decisions about course content and course delivery; secondly that wherever practically possible decisions about assessing a unit should be made within the context of the broader programme of study of which that unit is part. In other words it is desirable for departments to adopt a strategic overview of the overall 'diet' of assessment across the student experience. By standards we refer not only to the explicit expectations of student performance which are appropriate to the population addressed, measurable and achievable (see Boore, 1993) but also to the consistent and reliable implementation of those expectations.

Therefore the first priority for the subject centre is to address the issue of standards in the discipline by providing opportunities for sociologists to discuss common concerns in the collegial manner outlined by Pilkington et al in this volume. This might take the form of workshops where assessors practise designing rigorous and detailed assessment tasks and performance criteria by which student achievement is measured. In addition the subject centre should consider running events aimed at current and potential external examiners. Although many have argued that the external examiner system can no longer guarantee the standard of every script or coursework, others would argue their role remains critical though different. Clearly in a mass system few external examiners now see much more than a selected sample of student work. For this reason, many externals are now reluctant to alter individual marks – indeed regulations increasingly proscribe such arbitrary tinkering. However, many externals now play a more important role as overseer of provision, given that in a modular system they are likely to be the only person with that overview. This provides opportunities for external examiners to share their experiences in an informal setting. If Subject Centres take this task seriously they could play a key role in safeguarding the whole external examining system by making more robust our existing mechanisms for comparing standards.

The second function which the Subject Centre could perform would be as a 'buffer' between sociologists and the many external stakeholders involved in the regulatory framework. One example of this would be to play a key part in preparing Departments for the new system of Academic Review To an extent this process was set in motion in embryonic form during the recent consultations on subject benchmarking. Members of the Subject Benchmark Panel responded to requests to visit departments to explain the work of the Panel, to clarify the draft documents and to gather feedback. A second example would be to play a proactive role in liaising with both the BSA and ILT over the accreditation of university teachers.

The third area of concern for the new subject centre should be the ongoing issue of continuing professional development. If the higher education system continues to be subject to change and uncertainty then this could prove to be a valuable function. In doing this, the centre need look no further than the activities of other FDTL projects in sociology, for example the Sheffield based SSP2000 consortium, which was conspicuously successful in convening themed panels of academics to run workshops on 'teaching sociological theory', 'learning to research' and other issues of concern to the discipline. Another obvious base from which to build is the Open University based FDTL project which developed and piloted materials for use by part-time and postgraduate teachers of sociology.

More generally the subject centre has the opportunity to promote more scholarly approaches to the teaching and learning of sociology, including where appropriate, the process by which our students acquire sociological ways of thinking and reasoning. In doing this, it would be bringing British sociology into line with both cognate disciplines in the UK and belatedly mirroring the serious attention given to such issues by American sociology. Partly as a result of Sociology FDTL influence, the BSA conferences in 1999 and 2000 had, for the first time in many years, a conference stream dedicated to teaching and learning. The recently reformed committee structure of the BSA, most notably the establishment of a Professional Development committee, indicates a fresh preparedness to engage with such concerns.

Kogan (1988) differentiates between three types of accountability, to which higher education has been subjected. He distinguishes between managerial, professional and consumerist modes of accountability. These involve different kinds of discipline and are often in tension with one other. In addition the rhetoric of stakeholding brings into the debate a potentially unlimited audience with an interest in what sociologists teach and how they go about it. Railing against such processes is sociologically unsophisticated and politically naïve. Rather, we might see the future in terms of three challenges for sociology teachers. Firstly we need to make use of our own disciplinary concepts in an attempt to make sense of these apparently contradictory processes. Secondly, we need to see the unfolding tensions between state and universities as opportunities for critical engagement, not blind opposition. The final challenge is to begin to take the reproduction of the sociological curriculum as seriously as we take the production of social research.

Bibliography

Albrow, M. (1970), 'The Role of the Sociologist as Professional: The Case of Planning', in Halmos, P. (ed.) *The Sociology of Sociology*, Sociological Review Monograph, No. 16.

Albrow, M. (1986), 'The Undergraduate Curriculum in Sociology – "A core for humane education"', *Sociology*, 20(3), pp. 335–46.

Albrow, M. (1990), 'Skills and Capacities in the Sociology Curriculum', in Cross, M. and Payne, G. (eds.) *Sociology in Action*, Brighton: Falmer Press.

Ashcroft, K. and Palacio, D. (eds) (1996), *Researching into Assessment and Evaluation in Colleges and Universities*, London: Kogan Page.

Ashworth, A. and Harvey, R. (1994), *Assessing Quality in Further and Higher Education*, London: Jessica Kingsley.

Bailey, J. (1998), 'In Front of the Arras: Some New Introductions', *Sociology*, 32(1), pp. 203–9.

Baker, P. and Rau, W. (1990), 'The Cultural Contradictions of Teaching Sociology', in Gans, H. (ed.) *Sociology in America*, London: Sage.

Banks, J. A. (1971), *Sociology as a Vocation: An Inaugural Lecture*, Leicester: Leicester University Press.

Barnett, R. (1992), *Improving Higher Education*, Buckingham: Open University.

Baty, P. (2001), 'QAA rules tally climbs to 168', *The Higher*, January 26.

Becher, T. (1989), *Academic Tribes and Territories*, Buckingham: Open University Press.

Becher, T. (1994), 'The Significance of Disciplinary Differences', *Studies in Higher Education*, 19(2), pp.151–61.

Becher, T. and Kogan, M. (1992), *Process and Structure in Higher Education*, 2nd edition, London: Routledge.

Beyer, S. (1999), 'Gender differences in the accuracy of grade expectations and evaluations', *Sex Roles*, 41 (3/4): 279–290.

Boore, J. (1993), 'Teaching Standards from Quality Circles', in Ellis, R. (ed.), *Quality Assurance for University Teaching*, Buckingham: Open University Press.

Boud, D. (1997), *Enhancing Learning Through Self-Assessment*, London: Kogan Page.

Boud, D. and Miller, N. (eds.) (1996), *Working with Experience: animating learning*, London: Routledge.

Boud, D., Keogh, R. and Walker, D. (eds.) (1985), *Reflection: turning experience into learning*, London: Kogan Page.

153

Bradford, M. (1995), 'Common Core or Food for the Political Worm?', *Journal of Geography in Higher Education*, 19(1), pp. 5–9.

Broadfoot, P. (1990), 'Towards Curssessment: The Symbiotic Relationship between Curriculum and Assessment', in Entwistle, N. (ed.) *Handbook of Educational Ideas and Practice*, London: Routledge.

Brown, G. (1997), 'Teaching Psychology: a *vade mecum*' and responses, *Psychology Teaching Review*, 6(2), pp. 112–56.

Brown, S. and Glasner, A. (eds.) (1999), *Assessment Matters in Higher Education: Choosing and Using Diverse Approaches*, Buckingham: SRHE and Open University Press.

Brown, S and Knight, P. (1994), *Assessing Learners in Higher Education*, London: Kogan Page.

Brown, S., Race, P. and Smith, B. (1995), *500 Tips on Assessment*, London: Kogan Page.

Burgess, R. (1990), 'Sociologists, Training and Research', *Sociology*, 24(2), pp. 579–95.

Burgess, R. (ed.) (1994), *Postgraduate Education and Training in the Social Sciences: processes and products*, London: Jessica Kingsley.

Cave, M., Hannay, S., Kogan, M. and Trevett, G. (1988), *The Use of Performance Indicators in Higher Education: A Critical Analysis of Developing Practice*, London: Jessica Kingsley.

Clarke, J., Cochrane, A. and Mclaughlin, E. (eds) (1994), *Managing Social Policy*, London: Sage.

Cowan, J. (1998), *On Becoming an Innovative University Teacher*, Milton Keynes: Open University Press.

CVCP (1998), *Accreditation and Teaching in Higher Education, Final Report (The Booth Report)*, London: Committee of Vice Chancellors and Principals.

Dewey, J. (1981), 'Experience and Nature', in Boydson, J.A. (ed.) *John Dewey: the later works 1925–1953, Vol. I: 1925*, Carbondale: South Illinois University Press (Originally published 1925).

DfEE (1998), *A Common Framework for Learning*, London: DfEE.

Elias, N. (1994), *The Civilizing Process: the history of manners and state formation and civilization*, Oxford: Blackwell.

Evans, G. (1999), *Calling Academia to Account*, Buckingham: Open University Press.

Farnham, D. and Horton, S. (1996), *Managing the New Public Services*, London: MacMillan.

Fenton, S., Carter, J. and Modood, T. (2000), 'Ethnicity and Academia: Closure Models, Racism Models and Market Models', *Sociological Research Online*, 15(2).

Freeman, R. and Lewis, R. (1998), *Planning and Implementing Assessment*, London: Kogan Page.

Freire, P. (1972), *Pedagogy of the Oppressed*, Harmondsworth: Penguin.

George, J. and Cowan, J. (1999), *A Handbook of Techniques for Formative Evaluation*, London: Kogan Page.

Gibbs, G. (1981), *Teaching Students to Learn: A Student-Centred Approach*, Milton Keynes: Open University Press.

Gibbs, G. (1994), *Improving Student Learning: theory and practice*, Oxford: Oxford Centre for Staff Development.

Gibbs, G., Habeshaw, S. and Habeshaw, T. (1988), *53 Interesting Ways to Assess your Students*, Bristol: TES Ltd.

Giddens, A. (1990), *The Consequences of Modernity*, Cambridge: Polity.

Giddens, A. (1991), *Modernity and Self-Identity: Self and Society in the Late Modern Age*, Cambridge: Polity Press.

Gledhill, M. and Smith, P. (1996), *Student Perceptions of Learning with Reference to Group Work*, Buckinghamshire College Occasional Paper 12.

Gledhill, M. and Smith, P. (1997), *Student Perceptions and Learning*, Buckinghamshire College Occasional Paper 13.

Goldsmid, C. and Wilson, E. (1980), *Passing on Sociology: The Teaching of a Discipline*, California: Wadsworth.

Goodland, S. (1995), *The Quest for Quality*, Buckingham: Open University.

Gouldner, A. (1971), *The Coming Crisis of Western Sociology*, London: Heinemann.

Gubbay, J. (1993), 'Researching the Sociology Curriculum', in Cross, M. and Payne, G. (eds.) *Sociology in Action*, Basingstoke: Macmillan.

Halsey, A. H. (1992), *The Decline of Donnish Dominion*, Basingstoke: Macmillan.

Harrison, B. and Lyon, E.S. (1993), 'A Note on the Ethical Issues of Using Autobiography in Social Research', in *Sociology*, 27(1), pp. 101–109.

Harrison, B., Miller, N. and Powell, H. (2000), 'Assessing Autobiography' in Harrison, E. and Mears, R. (eds.)

Harrison, E. and Mears, R. (eds.) (2000), *Assessment Strategies in Sociology: A Resource Handbook*, Bath: Bath Spa University College.

HEFCE (1996), *Subject Overview Report – Sociology (Ref QO 8/96)*, London: Higher Education Funding Council for England.

HEFCE (2000), Transparency review reporting requirements, Circular Letter, no. 17/00, Bristol: Higher Education Funding Council.

Hood, C. O., James, G., and Jones C. Scott (2000), 'Regulation of Government: Has it Increased, Is It Increasing, Should It Be Diminished?', *Public Administration*, 78, 283–304.

Hood, C. O., James, G., Jones, C. Scott and Travers, T. (1998), *Regulation Inside Government: Waste Watchers Quality Police and Sleaze Busters*, Oxford: Oxford University Press.

Horn, R. (1998), *Peer Assessment*, Occasional Paper 17, Buckinghamshire Chilterns University College.

Horobin, G. and Davis, A. (eds.) (1977), *Medical Encounters: The Experience of Health and Illness*, London: Croom Helm.

Horton, M. (1990), *The Long Haul*, New York: Doubleday.

Hughes, G., Mears, R. and Winch, C. (1998), 'An Inspector calls; regulation and accountability in three public services', *Policy & Politics*, 25(3), pp. 299–313.

Illich, I. (1973), *Deschooling Society*, Harmondsworth: Penguin.

Inkeles, A. (1964), *What is Sociology? An Introduction to the Discipline and Profession*, New Jersey: Prentice Hall.

Janowitz, M. (1972), 'Professionalization of Sociology', *American Journal of Sociology*, 78(1), pp. 105-35.

Johnston, R. (1997), 'Graduateness' and a core curriculum for Geography?', *Journal of Geography in Higher Education*, 21(2), pp. 245–51.

Jordan, S. (1999), 'Self-assessment and peer assessment', pp. 172–182 in Brown and Glasner (eds).

Klein, R. (1990), 'From Status to Contract: the Transformation of the British Medical Profession', in Hugh L'Etang (ed), *Health Care Provision under Financial Constraint*, London, Royal Society of Medicine.

Knight, P. (2000), 'The value of a programme-wide approach to assessment', *Assessment and Evaluation in Higher Education*, 25(3).

Knight, P. T. and P.R. Trowler (2000), 'Departmental-level Cultures and the Improvement of Learning and Teaching', *Studies in Higher Education*, Vol. 25, No. 1.

Kogan, M. (1988), *Educational Accountability, An Analytic Overview*, 2nd edn, London, Hutchinson.

Lyon, E. S. (1998), 'The Teaching Quality Assessment in Sociology: did we do well?', *Network*, May.

Mahoney, P. and Zmroczek, C. (1997), *Class Matters: 'Working-Class' Women's Perspectives on Class*, London: Taylor and Francis.

Matthews, N. (1998), *Debating Gender and the Media*, Course Guide, and Teaching Methods Rationale Document (ECST LMO2 Doc C), Liverpool John Moores University (Unpublished).

Michelson, E. (1996), 'Beyond Galileo's telescope: situated knowledge and the assessment of experiential learning', in *Adult Education Quarterly*, 46(4), 185–196.

Miller, N. (1993a), 'How the T-group changed my life: a sociological perspective on experiential groupwork', in Boud, D., Cohen, R. and Walker, D. (eds.) *Using Experience for Learning*, Buckingham: SRHE and Open University Press.

Miller, N. (1993b), 'Autobiography and life history', in Miller, N. and Jones, D. (eds.) *Research: Reflecting Practice*, Boston: SCUTREA.

Mills, C. W. (1970), *The Sociological Imagination*, Harmondsworth: Penguin (Originally published 1959).

Morgan, D. (1998), 'Sociological Imaginings and Imagined Sociology: Bodies, Autobiographies and Other Mysteries', *Sociology*, 32(4), pp. 647–663.

Mouzelis, N. (1997), 'In Defence of the Sociological Canon: a reply to David Parker', *Sociological Review*, 45(2), pp. 244–53.

Neustadt, I. (1965), *Teaching Sociology: An Inaugural Lecture*, Leicester: Leicester University Press.

Oerton, S. (1999), 'Developments in Social Theory 2', Course Guide, University of Glamorgan (Unpublished).

O'Neill, J. (1972), *Sociology as a Skin Trade*, Heinemann: London.

Parker, D. (1997), 'Why Bother with Durkheim? Teaching Sociology in the 1990s', *Sociological Review*, 45(1), pp. 122–46.

Parker, M and Jary, D. (eds.) (1998), *The New Higher Education: Issues and Directions for the post-Dearing University*, Stoke-on-Trent, Staffordshire University Press.

Payne, G. (1998), 'Cohorts of Passive Sociologists?', *SSP 2000 Newsletter*, No. 2, October.

Pennington, G, (2000), 'Towards a New Professionalism: Accrediting Higher Education Teaching', in Fry, H., Ketteridge, S. and Marshall, S. (eds), *A Handbook for Teaching and Learning in Higher Education*, London: Kogan Page.

Pepper, D. and Webster, F. (1998), *The Assessment of Undergraduate Dissertations in the School of Social Sciences and Law*, Oxford Brookes University Occasional Paper.

Pilkington, A., Winch, C. and Leisten, R. (1999), *Dissertations in Sociology: Final Report*, University College Northampton Occasional Paper.

Platt, J. (1997), 'Progress report on the History of the BSA Project', *Network*, September.

Power, M. (1997), *The Audit Society*, Oxford: Oxford University Press.

Radford, J. (1997), 'Academic Psychologists: parasites, priests, proletariat or professionals?', *Psychology Teaching Review*, 6(2), pp. 170–80.

Ramsden, P. (1992), *Learning to Teach in Higher Education*, London: Routledge.

Reynolds, L. and Reynolds, J. (1970), *The Sociology of Sociology*, New York: David McKay.

Ribbens, J. (1991b), 'Writing Personally: Using autobiography within Undergraduate Coursework', *Teaching News* 29, Oxford Brookes University, Winter, pp. 5–8.

Ribbens, J. (1993), 'Facts or Fictions? Aspects of the Use of Autobiographical Writing in Undergraduate Sociology', *Sociology*, 27(1), pp. 81–92.

Ribbens, J. and students from Oxford Polytechnic (1991a), *The Personal and the Sociological: The Uses of Student Autobiography in Teaching Undergraduate Sociology*, Social Studies Department, Oxford Polytechnic.

Riley, M. (ed.) (1988), *Sociological Lives*, Newbury Park: Sage.

Scott, P. (1995), *The Meanings of Mass Higher Education*, Buckingham: Open University Press.

Silver, H. (1990), *A Higher Education, the Council for National Academic Awards and British Higher Education 1964–1989*, Brighton: Falmer Press.

Stacey, M. (1992), *Regulating British Medicine: The General Medical Council*, Chichester: Wiley.

Stanley, L. (1992), *The Auto/biographical I: The theory and practice of feminist autbiography*, Manchester: Manchester University Press.

Stewart, W. (1989), *Higher Education in Post-War Britain*, Basingstoke: Macmillan.

Thompson, A. (1998), *Undergraduate Life History Research Projects: Revised and Expanded Analysis of the History 2000 Questionnaire*, Unpublished report, University of Sussex.

Tight, M. (1988), 'So what is academic freedom?', in Tight, M. (ed) *Academic Freedom and Responsibility*, Milton Keynes: Open University Press.

Unwin, T. (1997), 'Rotten to the core: Against a Core Curriculum for Geography in UK Higher Education', *Journal of Geography in Higher Education*, 21(2), pp. 252–59.

Usher, R. and Edwards, R. (1994), *Postmodernism and Education*, London: Routledge.

Usher, R., Bryant, I. and Johnson, R. (1997), *Adult Education and the Postmodern Challenge. Learning beyond the limits*, London: Routledge.

Index